# INTERNATIONAL FOOTBALL BOOK

## *No. 21*

*A shot from West Germany v England 'B' game on the snow that marked last season.*

# INTERNATIONAL FOOTBALL BOOK

## *No. 21*

**Edited by Eric Batty**

with contributions by

KEVIN KEEGAN SEPP MAIER HANS KRANKL
DAVID O'LEARY JOHN WILE GLEN HODDLE
MARIAN MASNY GARY OWEN ARNOLD MÜHREN
MIKE THOMAS PHIL NEAL GORDON COWANS
VIV ANDERSON

*SOUVENIR PRESS LTD LONDON*

*First published 1979 by Souvenir Press Ltd, 43, Great Russell Street, London WC1B 3PA, and simultaneously in Canada*

*ISBN 0 285 62401 6*

*Filmset by BAS Printers Limited, Over Wallop, Hampshire and printed in Great Britain by J. W. Arrowsmith Ltd., Bristol*

CONTENTS

## LIST OF ILLUSTRATIONS

*Photographs provided by*
Sporting Pictures (UK) Ltd.,
7a, Lambs Conduit Passage,
Holborn,
London WC1.

# DAVID O'LEARY THINKS EIRE CAN STILL BEAT ENGLAND IN THE EUROPEAN CHAMPIONSHIP

★ ★ ★ ★ ★

I was born in London and play for a London club, but my father was Irish and when I was only a few weeks old my family moved to Glasnevin, just outside Dublin, and I spent all my childhood in Ireland.

My first senior club was Shelbourne, a famous old Irish club and I began playing for them in their Under 12 team, and moved up through the club to the Under 15 side.

Then, with Manchester United interested in me, I was approached by Gordon Clarke, now helping Queens Park Rangers, but at that time working for Arsenal.

*Pat Jennings, seen in action above, 'is so reliable', says his Arsenal colleague David O'Leary, pictured on the ball (facing page)*

After spending two weeks on trial with Manchester United they were humming and ha-ing, but Mr. Clarke was very keen for me to sign for Arsenal, so I made up my mind and joined them.

Signing as an apprentice professional for Arsenal when I was fifteen, it will probably come as a shock to many youngsters of today to know that at that time I received only £6 a week.

Bertie Mee was the Arsenal manager at that time, and I was very fortunate to get an early chance to play in the first team. I had my first game in a Testimonial match at Reading when I was only sixteen, and then I was seventeen and a few months when I played for Arsenal away to Burnley.

Mr. Mee told me not to expect to keep my place because he felt that I might tire physically, being so young, and though I was too busy enjoying myself to keep the score, I was told later that I then played thirty consecutive games for Arsenal before I lost my place through an injury.

The present Arsenal team is really a very good one and well balanced. Pat Jennings is so reliable in goal and Liam Brady had an exceptional run last season. He really is a fantastic player.

Up front we had Frank Stapleton and Alan Sunderland knocking in goals, but it is probably unfair really to single out individuals because the general standard is so high, and every one is a good player in his own right.

Strangely enough, although I have become aware of Arsenal's great traditions, it is only through the players that have been transferred to the club that I have been really made aware of it. I remember when Malcolm MacDonald signed for us, he told me 'Arsenal are a great club, a big name. Everyone wants to beat them'. But to me, having been with the club since I was fifteen, I find it difficult to understand, and I don't feel any pressure at all from the club's golden days.

*Liam Brady (facing page) is a fantastic player writes David O'Leary, who says he was only made really aware of Arsenal's great traditions when the club signed Malcolm MacDonald (photo left), who told him 'Everyone wants to beat Arsenal'*

Every year I hope to improve my game, and for example, last season I think I began to read the game better, which is very important for a centre back. Then again I have always been encouraged to get upfield and do things at the other end of the field, and I felt I was beginning to understand better last season what was involved.

The Arsenal coach, Don Howe, keeps on at all of us with two favourite expressions—'do not underestimate anyone' . . . and . . . 'You are only as good as your last game'.

I think these two points, or something very similar must be driven home to the Liverpool players too, for I have come to really appreciate Don Howe's preaching and I think I am becoming more consistent as a result. At least I hope so, and I certainly work hard to achieve it.

You have to admire Liverpool, for every year they run off with one or two honours. Two European Cup successes and the League championship, year in, year out, they have the consistency that we are after at Highbury.

Other clubs have won the League or the Cup and then followed it with a poor season, but that just doesn't seem to happen at Liverpool.

Although I am a professional I still enjoy playing and I have had very many enjoyable matches. But the biggest special game for me so far was our FA Cup semi-final in 1978, when we beat Orient 3–0. The final whistle in that game gave me tremendous pleasure, for it meant that I was going to play in the Cup Final.

Of course we were beaten at Wembley by Ipswich, but the 1977–78 season was quite a good one for Arsenal, for we also did well enough in the League to earn a place in the UEFA Cup.

I thought we had a good chance to do well in that competition, and I think we would have too, had Liam Brady not been suspended for our matches against Red Star, Belgrade.

After disposing of Lokomotive Leipzig, we met Hajduk Split, a team that I had a very high regard for. We had met them when I was just travelling with the squad as a reserve in a pre-season friendly, and they were extremely good at that time. Because I remembered them as such a good side, I was disappointed with them when we came to play them, for they had lost a few of their best players who had gone abroad, and we won without too much trouble.

But in that match Liam Brady was sent off, which led to his suspension for the next round. I did not see the incident that led up to Brady pushing the Yugoslav away, but that was all he did. And off he went. It really was a travesty of justice for Brady took 85 minutes of real stick before pushing the Yugoslav. This fellow had really tight-marked Brady, following him everywhere and continually fouling him. The referee should have sorted the Yugoslav out, but he didn't and in the end it was Brady that suffered.

*Action (facing page) from last season's UEFA cup games against Hajduk Split (above) and Red Star, who eliminated Arsenal. Pictured above is Arsenal coach Don Howe, who, says O'Leary, drives him to consistent performances by preaching 'do not underestimate anyone'*

FUJI FILM

*Trevor Francis, now with Nottingham Forest (photo left) 'is one of the best strikers in Britain, really very sharp and quick with the ball on the ground' says David O'Leary. Having cost Forest £1 million, he ought to be!*

I thought we could have gone a long way in the UEFA Cup for as things turned out, the two continental teams I had the greatest respect for were AC Milan and Valencia, and they were both very disappointing.

But our hopes ended against Red Star, and I didn't think they were as good as Hajduk, and with Brady playing I feel sure we would have eliminated them.

I did like Red Star's midfield player Vladimir Petrovic. He was very gifted, and coming to Highbury with only a 1–0 lead I must admit that they did very well to draw. They were very professional, and very experienced. They had to be, to defend a one goal lead successfully. We had enough chances to have won convincingly, but near the end their centre forward Dusan Savic took a good goal to earn a draw, and we were out.

Savic was not a specially good player, rather like an English type centre forward. But generally I think the Yugoslavs play a type of football that is very much like our game. Certainly they are more like the English in the physical sense than any other continental country.

I think some of the Yugoslavs could do well in England, and I am all in favour of allowing foreigners to play here. I know the critics argue that foreign players would limit the chances of English youngsters, but I believe the class will come through if the English players are good enough.

Foreigners in the English game can only improve our football. After all, if foreign teams can sign our top players like Kevin Keegan, why should we not be allowed to do the same?

The big problem for foreign players would be, can they adjust their play to the demands of English football?

One player that would do well here is Ruud Krol of Ajax and Holland. He is past his best now, but he is a class player.

The Argentinian Mario Kempes also looked very good in the World Cup and I think he would do well in England too.

As Don Howe says, you must never under-estimate anyone, but in England there are several players who are difficult for me to handle as a central defender.

Trevor Francis is one of the best strikers in Britain, really very sharp, and very quick with the ball on the ground.

Andy Gray of Aston Villa is another very dangerous striker, a good all round player and very dangerous in the air.

Abroad, Johan Cruyff and Franz Beckenbauer were probably the classiest players of my time, so good to watch. But I also liked George Best at his best, for he was a very exciting player.

On the continent generally, I think the West German Bundesliga has offered the highest standard of play, but last season I think the standard dropped there a bit. So West Germany, Spain and Italy are probably the most difficult continental leagues to play in, and I think the Italians could be specially prominent in the European competitions if they decided to allow foreigners into Italy again. Obviously money is no object in Italy, and they would sign many of the very best players available.

As well as playing for Arsenal I am also lucky enough to be involved in international football with the Republic of Ireland. Our manager Johnny Giles has done a great job in lifting Eire from being an ordinary team, and we have a very good side now.

What Mr. Giles has done is to get all the players to believe in the kind of football he wants played. He also has the knack of bringing on good young players and giving them confidence. Mark Lawrenson of Brighton has played very well for us and I am sure he will become an outstanding performer.

Of course we have some established stars too in Gerry Daly and Steve Heighway, as well as my Arsenal colleagues, Liam Brady and Frank Stapleton.

Altogether I am very optimistic about the future.

But you need the breaks to be successful at international level, especially away from home. I thought for example that we could have qualified for the 1978 World Cup. But in our game away to Bulgaria the referee had a stinker, and very many of his decisions puzzled me. As I said you need the breaks at top level, and if we had got them I think we could have qualified instead of France.

*Brighton's Mark Lawrenson (photo above right) has impressed O'Leary while playing for the Republic of Ireland, and the Arsenal star tips him to become an outstanding player in the near future*

In Dublin, against England, we wanted to win very badly. But it was a strange game in which one side were on top for about twenty minutes and then the other side took control for a while. Both sides had good chances, but neither team played well enough to deserve to win, and in my opinion a 1–1 draw was a fair result.

Hopefully I still think that we can qualify for the last eight, but it will not be easy. It is a very tight group, and Northern Ireland did very well to win 2–0 against Bulgaria in Sofia. I am sure that both Eire and England will find it difficult to win in Sofia, and probably the group winners will not be known until after the final game in the group. But, with a little luck I think we can still make it.

# FOREIGN PLAYERS COULD BE GOOD FOR ENGLISH FOOTBALL

*says*

**SEPP MAIER**

THE WEST GERMAN GOALKEEPER

*Sepp Maier (portrait above) and facing page, down at the feet of Johan Cruyff*

I know that since English clubs began to engage foreign players there has been great discussion about it. Many people seem to be very firmly against the principle, but here in Germany, our clubs are allowed two foreign players each and they make a big contribution to the success of the Bundesliga teams.

In my opinion the foreign stars we have lend wings to our game, and lift it up. Players like Allan Simonsen, the Dane who plays for Borussia Mönchengladbach, and Kevin Keegan of Hamburg SV are world class, and they draw big crowds wherever they play. That can only be good for the game.

Keegan, I would say, is the *commander* of the Hamburg team and they rise and fall with him. If Keegan plays well then HSV are very, very difficult to beat, but they are not half the side they can be when he has an off day or a quiet game.

*Allan Simonsen, the Danish striker of Borussia Mönchengladbach (facing page) is one of the foreign players who 'lend wings to German football' says Sepp Maier, pictured below with the European Cup he helped to win three times with FC Bayern München.*

erdgas

Foreigners have been a problem in Italy for example, but that was because the clubs signed too many of them. There was no limit in Italy during the fifties and even the poorer teams signed some South Americans. The crack teams like AC Milan and Juventus had almost half a team of foreigners each, and obviously when you reach that point then it must be faced that imported players are preventing good home born players from gaining the vital experience at top level. So the national team can suffer. That is what happened in Italy, but they went too far when they banned foreign players altogether.

Getting the right balance is important in everything, and as I see it, two foreigners for each team is probably about right.

Anyway, foreign players are certainly no problem in Germany, and I think that the English game could benefit too, as long as there is a low limit like ours, on the numbers.

Football has been very good to me and I have a host of fine memories. I have been lucky enough to help win all the major trophies that Bayern Munich and West Germany could win. European Cup Finals, even the World Cup and the European Nations Cup, and Cups and League championships in Germany. My cup is full, but if I have one truly great memory it was beating England 3–1 at Wembley in what I think was the best German team we ever had.

Winning at Wembley was fantastic and making the pleasure even sweeter, it was the quarter-final of the European championship which we went on to win, beating Russia 3–0 in the final in Brussels. The team we had then was a really great side without a weakness anywhere, and we had a lot of what you call 'flair' in the side too. Players like Gerd Müller, Gunter Netzer and Franz Beckenbauer, were all at the top of their profession.

Of course every country has its ups and downs. I know England had a bad patch and failed to qualify for the 1978 World Cup, but these things go in cycles, and I am sure England are on the way up again.

After all our successes in recent years we had a disastrous 1978 and it was so unexpected because though we lost Franz Beckenbauer when he went to the United States, we still had a lot of very good players and a good, well balanced team.

But still things went wrong in Argentina. We cannot offer any excuses either for everything there was just fine. The people were very friendly and I liked the country generally, but somehow we managed to get ourselves into a mess.

Nothing seemed to work for us, but I am sure our World Cup team was really much better than it looked. No one could explain what went wrong, but we just never got going. All the players were keyed up for it, but it didn't work out. I still have nightmares even now, about our 2–3 beating against Austria, and I simply cannot explain how it happened.

But in football you just have to play your way through these critical periods and I believe we have started to do it.

At the start of last season I resolved to put all thoughts of Argentina behind me, and things began to work out again.

With Bayern I had a good season. We had a very useful team and did well, but it is not easy to win the championship in Germany. Maybe we can do it next season, but the competition is very fierce today.

One thing I would like to do is to help Bayern win the UEFA Cup, and if our present side is not as good as past teams, we could if things went right for us, carry off this trophy. I certainly hope Bayern can do it in my time.

I have signed a new contract with Bayern and hope to go on playing for several years yet. There is no reason to quit just because you reach a certain age, and as long as I do not get a serious injury I will go on playing. When the time to give up comes I am sure I will know it, for I have always enjoyed playing football, and when the element of fun is gone, then I will know it is time to quit.

We have some very good players in the Bayern side. Paul Breitner is back after playing in Spain for Real Madrid, and playing really well too. Then we have Karl-Heinz Rummenigge who prefers outside right but can also play on the other wing, and he is very talented. I am sure he will be a great player and become known everywhere.

*Inside right Gunter Netzer (left) who was one of the biggest stars in Maier's truly great memory—beating England 3–1 at Wembley in 1972, and, photo right, his Bayern München colleague, Karl-Heinz Rummenigge 'who will surely become known everywhere'*

After the World Cup our new manager, Jupp Derwall, paid me a great compliment by appointing me captain of the German team. It was a great honour and I was very happy about it personally. But I am sure it will not last. Having a goalkeeper as the captain is not ideal, because he is too far away from most of the team.

If one of the players makes a few mistakes, it helps if the captain can give him a few words of comfort and encouragement, and of course in goal that is not always possible. So my appointment had to be a temporary thing.

For Germany I will go on playing as long as I am chosen, and I hope at least to keep my place for the finals of the 1980 European Championship in Italy.

The new team that arose from the ashes of Argentina is developing into a good side. In fact we played very well even in our first games after the World Cup disaster.

The team is a good mixture of old, experienced players, and youngsters with a lot of talent. It is already a strong side again, with a lot of enthusiasm, and I am sure we will be back amongst the strongest European teams very quickly.

The backbone of the new team is provided by players like my Bayern colleague Rummenigge who is a real find, and centre forward Klaus Fischer who has once more found his goalscoring touch.

In the defence the strong man is Manfred Kaltz from Hamburg SV. He is a fine player and already experienced enough at top level, and at 26 he is young enough to improve still further.

I am the old man of the side at 35 and I suppose my days are numbered. But as I have already said I hope to keep my place until after the 1980 competition in Italy. But I know it will not be easy for we have several very good goalkeepers in their mid twenties.

Tennis has always been a passion with me though of course I am not professional class, but I really get a great deal of pleasure from the game. I have invested a lot of the money I have made from football in a big indoor and outdoor tennis centre in Munich, and the facilities are such that people can come and play there all the year round, regardless of the weather.

When I give up playing football I am not sure whether I would like to stay in the game as a coach. In any case, running my tennis centre has taken up all my free time since it was built, for there is a lot to do there.

As I have already said, I would like to play for Germany until 1980 and help Bayern win the UEFA Cup, but my secret ambition is to play Björn Borg at Wimbledon . . . . just for fun.

*Klaus Fischer (above) of Schalke O4 who appears to have settled in at number nine for West Germany, and, facing page, Sepp Maier's 'dream' opponent, Björn Borg, the Swedish tennis ace.*

5
15
3

# PLAYING AT WEMBLEY
# I WOULD LIKE

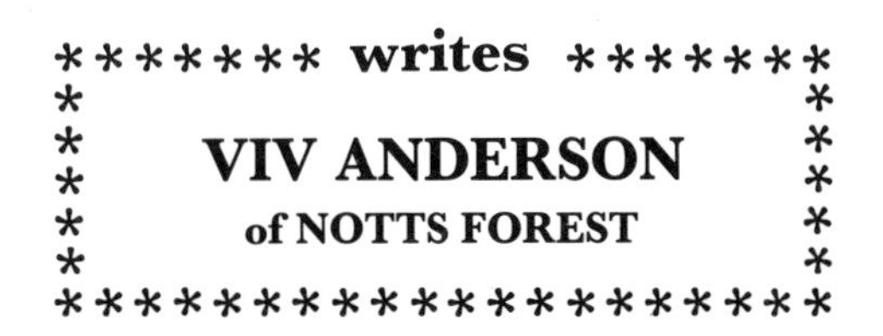
writes
VIV ANDERSON
of NOTTS FOREST

*Viv Anderson, portrait (left) was first capped at 21, and with his consistent league form could become a regular choice for England. On the right is a photo of the Forest Squad that won the First Division championship in season 1977–78*

# IS GREAT . . .

# TO DO IT EVERY WEEK

ONE of the biggest thrills in my career so far was to be named by Ron Greenwood for the England team to meet Czechoslovakia. I was thrilled to be in the side, delighted to play, and of course it was extra nice to be on the winning side on my debut.

At the time the newspapers made a lot of fuss over the fact that I was the first coloured player to represent England, but honestly, it didn't mean anything to me at the time. It was some time later when it sunk in that my name will go down in the history books, because of my colour. But I would prefer to be remembered for the way I played.

Having made my debut for England when only 21, naturally I hope to be chosen a few more times, and I would be delighted if I could earn a regular place in the side.

I had played at Wembley before of course, for Notts Forest in the Football League Cup Final against Liverpool, and also in the F.A. Charity Shield match at the start of the 1978–79 season. But playing at Wembley is always a special experience. Just being there is a thrill that I think is unique in the game, and playing there is fantastic.

It is difficult to explain just what is special about Wembley. Obviously the atmosphere is tremendous and I have found it stimulating as a player. It is the atmosphere of course, but also something more that I cannot define. Whatever it is, I'd like to play there every week.

Playing against Liverpool at Anfield has something of the atmosphere of Wembley, but only to a certain degree, and whatever it is that Wembley has, I certainly feel it, and it really is special.

I thought Czechoslovakia were a very good side and they played particularly well in the first half when they adapted themselves to the conditions far better than England did. But we changed our game a little in the second half, put on the pressure then, and I think we just about deserved to win.

*Viv Anderson in action (right) against Czechoslovakia and pictured on the left, John Robertson, 'who' says Anderson 'is difficult to mark because he drops deep to work in midfield'.*

The best winger I have ever faced so far is probably Scotland's Willie Johnston. He is skilful and intelligent, and also very quick, not only over the first few yards which is vital, but over twenty or thirty yards too. So against him you have to make your first challenge count. To be beaten is the road to trouble.

There are not too many natural left wingers about, but one of the best is surely John Robertson, my colleague at Forest. I play against him in training games and he makes life difficult for full backs because he drops so deep looking for the ball, and working in midfield.

You cannot tight mark wingers like John because a full back has other duties in defence, and he would pull you out of position if you tried to follow him. So when he gets the ball and comes at you, it is easy to get into trouble. He is a very good dribbler, with two good feet and able to pass you on either side. So in a one v one situation, you never know which way he is going and he is also very nippy over the first ten yards.

Although there are obviously times when you stand or fall on your own ability, I am sure my play has developed, at least in part, to the fact that I have played regularly with a lot of good players at club

To play regularly for England would be a tremendous boost to my career for this would bring me into opposition with some of the world's top players. I have met some of them already, for Forest in the European Cup, and hope to go on playing in European competition with them too.

Once you have reached a fairly high level in the game, the way you improve after that is by playing against really top quality players. There is no substitute for this experience, and learning from really good opponents is the way to the top.

*Willie Johnston of West Brom and Scotland is the best winger Viv Anderson has faced so far (photo above), and pictured on the right, goalkeeper Peter Shilton, who has played a vital role in Forest's successful run*

*John McGovern and Archie Gemmill display the Charity Shield that Forest won in 1978*

level. Without exception, everyone at Forest has helped me, because if you are having a bad game everyone tries to help you with words of advice. Above all they all encourage you to keep going, which is vitally important when you have an off day.

I was only 19 when I first got in the side, and young and inexperienced it can be a terrible experience to have a bad game that takes a lot out of your confidence. But with Forest, I have never had anything but help and encouragement from everyone.

Obviously we have a lot of very good players at Forest, but in my opinion the backbone of the side are Peter Shilton, Archie Gemmill, Kenny Burns, John Robertson and Tony Woodcock. Surrounded by players of their class, it is relatively easy to play well.

Goal scoring full backs have been a feature of the game in recent years and I have been fortunate to score a few myself. I think the most important goal I scored for Forest was my first one, but not many people will remember that. It was in a Second Division match against Sheffield United in my early days in the first team.

The best goal, the most satisfying to me, was one I got in a Football League cup tie against Everton last season. At the time the score was 1–1, and I got the ball some way out and set off on a run. Near the edge of the penalty area, with a couple of Everton players close by, I let fly and it bent in. That put us 2–1 up, and we went on to win 3–1.

Although goals are far from easy to come by in the First Division, goal scoring has always been part of the game for me, because in fact I started out as a centre forward.

I was born in Nottingham on 29th July, 1956. My parents came to England from Jamaica, and in fact though my father was a keen cricketer he never played football. They do play in Jamaica of course and I well remember seeing young boys playing in the park when I was in Jamaica.

We didn't see any organised football, but while I remember some things very clearly, other memories are hazy, because on my only visit I was just twelve years old. I may be wrong, but it seemed to me that life in Jamaica was very fast, and I didn't like it. I feel much more at home in Nottingham.

Like all English boys I began to play football when I was very young. It was probably around six or seven years of age that I started and I was quite successful as a youngster. I played for the Nottingham Schoolboys Representive side and also for the County Schoolboys team.

But if I always had ambitions about the game, my opportunity came comparatively late. I was 17 years old and playing for a senior amateur club, when a Forest scout, the late Ernie Roberts, saw me play and asked if I would like a trial. Naturally I jumped at the chance, and after several trial games I was offered an apprenticeship. Being a late comer, that only lasted for one year and when I was 18 I signed as a full time professional. I know that many 18 year olds earn far more today, but I was very satisfied to be in the game at 18, even if I was earning only about £25 a week.

Forest converted me from a goal scoring centre forward to right back, and of course I had to start again, almost from scratch, learning how to be a good defender.

Outside the game I enjoy all sports, with a particular liking for tennis and squash. Of course I am only a keen amateur but I play as often as I can. I just play for pleasure, with a little bet on the side to give the game a little more of a competitive zest.

But my real enthusiasm is for football. I do enjoy playing of course but being a professional, it isn't all just fun like tennis and squash are. But having helped Forest to promotion, won a championship medal and another one in the Football League Cup, all before I was 20, I just want to go on playing and hopefully, help the trophies to keep coming to the City Ground.

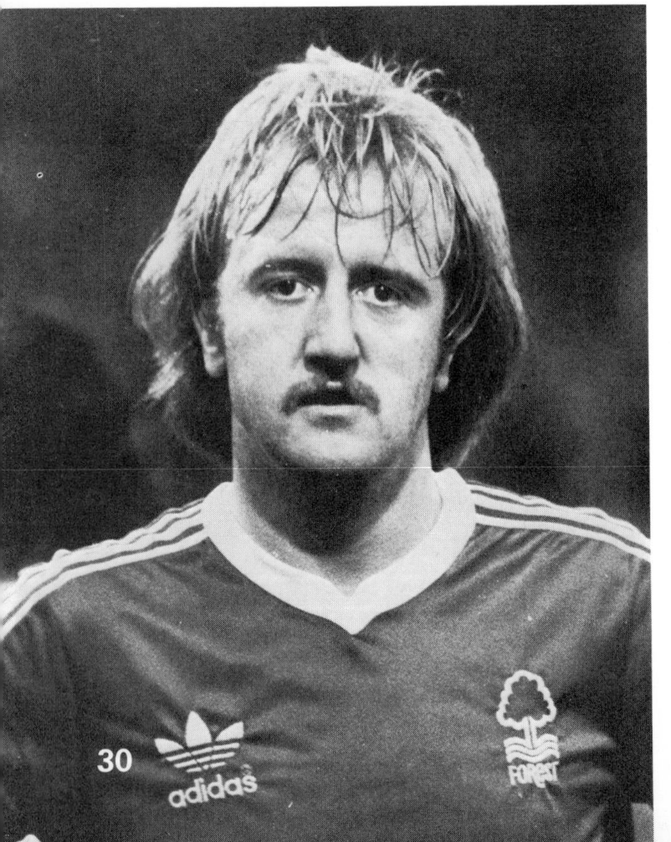


*Tony Woodcock in action (facing page) and, on the left Kenny Burns who was voted 'Footballer of the Year in 1978'*

## AWARDED TO

# KEVIN KEEGAN

### OF ENGLAND AND HAMBURG SV

**'A DIFFERENT TEMPERAMENT IS REQUIRED TO SUCCEED IN GERMAN, AS COMPARED TO ENGLISH FOOTBALL' WRITES KEVIN KEEGAN**

*Kevin Keegan (portrait left) is pictured on the right winning a tussle with Liam Brady in the 1–1 draw between England and Eire in Dublin.*

THE game in West Germany's Bundesliga is very different from that played in England. For one thing the Germans use a *libero* playing free behind the defence and he stays deep, so that there is virtually never an off-side decision.

There are almost no high crosses in the German game either, but lots of one-two's and close passing movements.

Some people believe that the continentals play more slowly, but this isn't true in Germany, although it is just as quick as in England, but in a different way. The Germans play it very quickly around the penalty box, knocking off the ball and sprinting into the area looking for the one-two back—and in for a shot.

By comparison, I feel that more of the English game is concentrated in mid-field, where, by and large, most games are won and lost. In England you

*Kevin Keegan in action (facing page) for Hamburg SV and below, shouting instructions to a colleague in the West Germany v England match in February 1978*

HS

can sometimes find as many as eighteen or twenty players concentrated in mid-field, and whichever side gains control, they usually win.

Overall I think that the English and the West German Leagues are the two best in the world, and the level of skills in both leagues is comparable too.

Asked to decide which league is better I wouldn't like to make an overall judgement, but I have found that the German game suits me better. I liked playing for Liverpool and I enjoy playing for Hamburg, but because the Germans always pair off for individual duels in their man for man marking system, I really enjoy the cut and thrust of each personal duel in the games. I enjoy the personal challenge to come out on top of the man marking me. You might say it gives me job satisfaction.

There are a lot of players in England who could come out to German clubs and do very well for themselves. Very many that I can think of have the necessary ability to star in Germany, but I think a lot would struggle with things like the language barrier and the fact that a different temperament is required to succeed in Germany, as compared to English football.

The Germans also have a lot of good players who could do well in England but I think the Germans would have more problems with English clubs. For a start it is a different game, and they would have to adjust; but more important, they are not accustomed to playing in mid-week, often for weeks on end, and overall playing more than sixty matches a season. The Germans would probably not have the physical condition, the strength and stamina, to play well twice a week.

If the Hamburger Sport Verein is typical then training in Germany is very different to what I was accustomed to with Liverpool. At Anfield we trained five times a week if there was no mid-week match, and had Sunday off.

Every day we used to train for one and a half to two hours, working very hard one day early in the week, with a lot of hard running. Overall we gradually worked down as the week progressed, definitely a much slower tempo on Thursdays, and doing very little on Fridays so that all the players had plenty of energy for the game on Saturday.

With Hamburg there is no day off. Playing on Saturdays, we go in on Sundays for a sauna bath and massage. Then on Monday afternoon, starting at 3 p.m. we have a practice game.

On Tuesdays we train twice. In the morning from 9 till 10 we have a very strenuous hour in a gymnasium, and then in the afternoon, again at three o'clock, we have one hour of hard running.

Wednesday is usually a fairly hard day with quite hard training followed by a game, again in the afternoon.

Thursday is another two session day and both morning and afternoon the emphasis is on ball work, working at skills and shooting etc. Then on Friday we train harder than was customary with Liverpool, and then off to a hotel before the game on Saturday.

I am sure that I have improved my skills with Hamburg, first because we have more time to work at them because a mid-week match is rare. Then again, I have learned better how to cope with one *v* one situations and I hope that I am better at taking people on now. With more time to work at skills, and facing man to man marking in every match, you can hardly fail to improve.

As a result I feel generally more confident now about taking a man on, but in one respect I think I have lost something. Because there are not so many crosses in Germany, I think I have lost a bit in terms of heading ability.

The HSV coach, Branko Zebec, is a Yugoslav and he works us very hard. I think we must be the fittest team in Europe!

*'I am sure I have improved my skill while with Hamburg, because we spend more training time working at skills and shooting' says Kevin Keegan. 'But because there are not so many crosses in Germany I think I have lost a bit in terms of heading ability' but as the photo on the right recalls, Keegan beat Pat Jennings in the air to head the first goal in England's 4–0 victory over Northern Ireland*

Then again he has lots of very good ideas and generally gets the players to improve all round. For example, if a player tends to run, only when he has got the ball, and doesn't run to take up good positions off the ball, then our coach produces exercises with the ball and a group of players, to *make* them run off the ball. Like everything else, this improves with constant practice.

It has been put to me that in England, players take time to settle down with the England team, and I would agree with this. Personally I would write off my first fourteen or fifteen England games because I didn't feel at the time that I did myself justice.

There are exceptions of course and one of them was Peter Barnes, who came in for his first cap in the vital World Cup qualifier at Wembley against Italy, and did very well. But I think that overall, though I hope it doesn't happen to Peter, those that do well for England very quickly, generally seem to fade out of the picture earlier.

It seems to me that playing for England is very different from League football and there is a kind of barrier that each player has to go through.

As far as I am concerned, I think that at one stage I felt that I had finally played as well as I could for England, and having had a good game, confidence

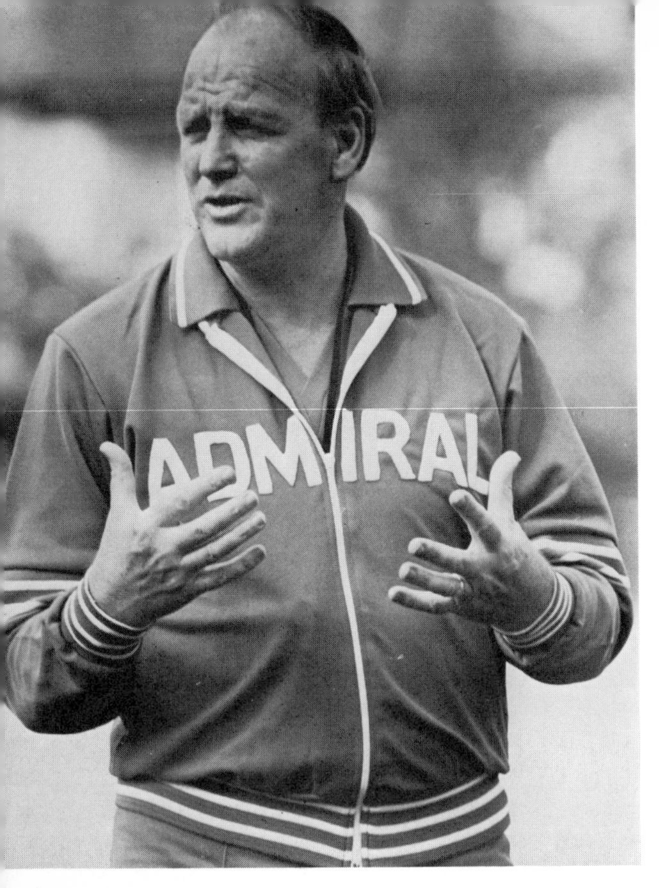


comes and you settle down. I have been most pleased with my last few games for England, doing myself justice at last.

With England, Mr. Greenwood has an approach all his own. He gives the individual player much more lee-way and I am sure the other players feel as I do and try to give it back to him. Certainly I would hate to feel that I ever let Ron Greenwood down. And that can only be good for the England team in the near future.

Although I am very happy now with Hamburg and not long ago signed a new contract to play for them in 1979–80, I felt in the early months that four or five times, I was close to wanting to go back home.

I had the definite feeling that the bulk of the Hamburg players did not think that they needed new players and I got the distinct impression that they did not want me.

The Yugoslav international, Ivan Buljan, was not very well accepted either, and the HSV manager of the time did not do much to help me.

The arrival of the former German inside forward star, Gunter Netzer, finally made the club for me. He took over as the manager—business manager—during the summer of 1978.

Gunter Netzer has to be a good business man to hold down the job of course, but in addition, he understands football and he also gets on very well with the players.

Adjusting to the way of life in Germany was not difficult. Outside the game I liked the food and the people, and while my wife Jean could speak German, I had to learn the language and I enjoyed that as a new challenge.

The Germans do have a different mentality to the English and though I like living with them, I have to agree with what I had heard, the Germans do work harder than the English.

As a player, I should feel that players ought to have freedom of contract like almost everyone else in the entertainment industry. But I can see that it would not be good for the game.

I feel that the system the Germans have; of relating transfer fees to salaries, is a very good one, and is perhaps the best compromise that one could get for the game.

When a German player is transferred, his club cannot ask a fee of more than five times his contracted salary. So if a player is earning £100,000 a year, his club can ask a transfer fee, if he moves, of five times that amount. That is £500,000.

So if another player is only paid £10,000 a year, his club cannot ask more than £50,000 for him if he changes clubs.

That rule encourages the clubs to pay the players the maximum that they can afford, knowing that when the time comes for him to go, they will be able to ask a higher transfer fee.

So the German rules ensure that the players are very well paid.

*England manager, Ron Greenwood (photo above) 'gives the players more lee-way, and the players have responded', says Kevin Keegan. 'Certainly I would hate to feel that I ever let him down' he adds*

# MANCHESTER IS FULL OF FOOTBALL FANATICS

says

**MIKE THOMAS**

**Manchester United and Wales**

*Mike Thomas celebrates another goal for Manchester United*

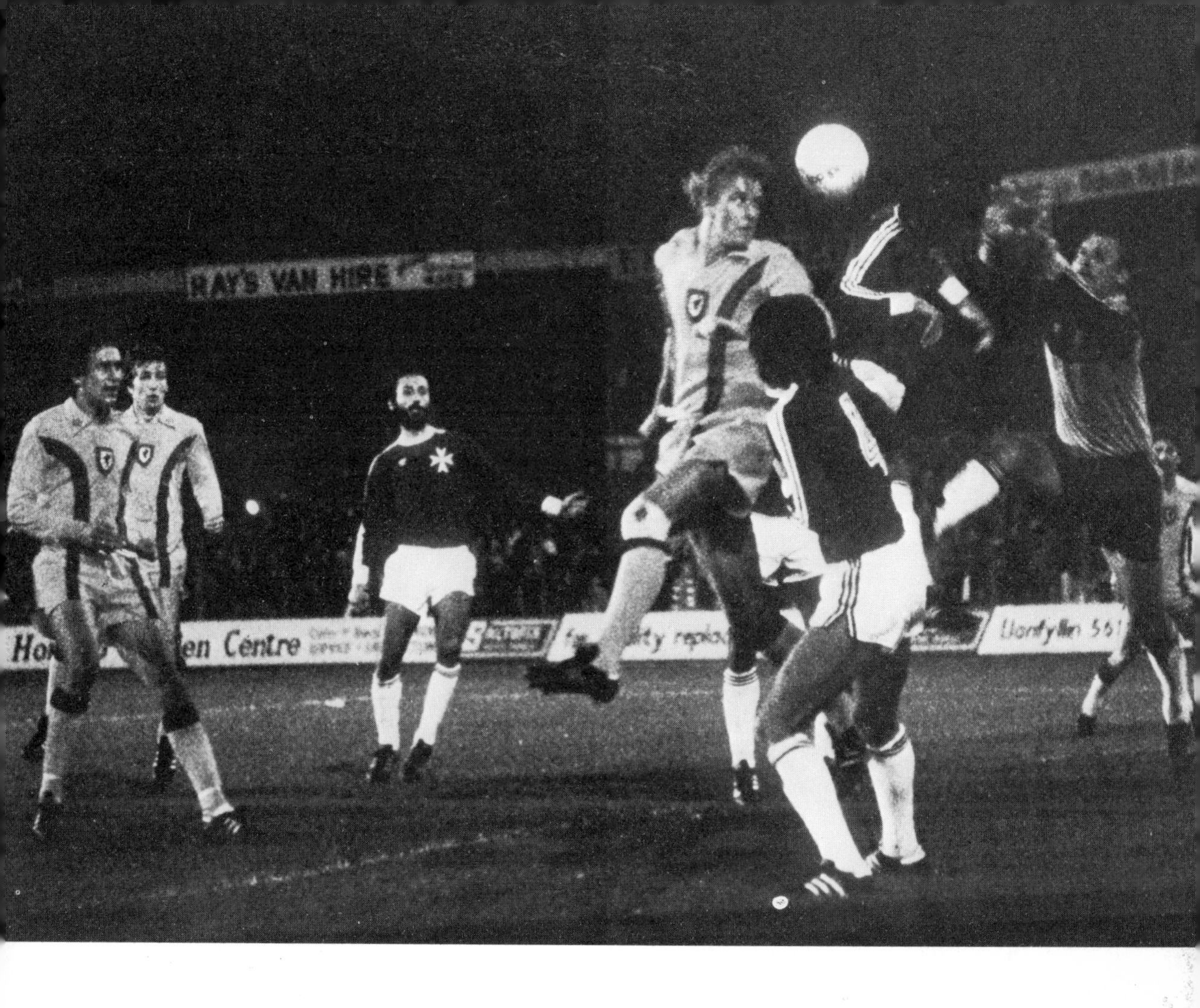


*Mike Thomas was signed by Wrexham after having a trial in Llandudno and in the same game Wrexham discovered Joey Jones (in action, facing page). Photo above shows goalmouth action in the 7–0 win that Wales recorded against Malta last season.*

COLWYN Bay is not a Welsh rugby playing area, but neither is it strong football country either, but that is where I was born on the 7th of July, 1954. I owe my chance to become a professional with Wrexham, and my transfer to Manchester United to the fact that the Welsh club holds trials every year in North Wales.

When I was fourteen I was invited by the Wrexham scout Evan Williams to a trial at Llandudno, and then, fortunately, I was invited to sign schoolboy forms for Wrexham. Playing in that same trial, and also signing for Wrexham was Wales and former Liverpool left back Joey Jones.

When I left school at fifteen I became an apprentice with Wrexham, and my first taste of international football came for the Welsh amateur Youth team.

I played for them against Northern Ireland at Bangor, when we won 3–2, and later I also played for the Welsh professional Youth team.

With Wrexham I finally helped the club win promotion to Division Two for the 1978–79 season, but then after playing twenty games I was transferred to Manchester United.

Going almost at one step from the Third Division to the First is a big jump but having played international football for Wales, it was not too difficult to adjust. In my first game for Manchester United Sammy McIlroy was a big help, for he is a great talker during the game, and it helped me a lot.

Dave McCreery and I struck up an immediate friendship too, and in fact I stayed with him while I was looking for somewhere to live in the Manchester area. Dave is a very useful player, and a very nice man into the bargain.

Life in a big city like Manchester is a far cry from a small town like Wrexham, and I found it quite difficult to adjust at first. And Manchester is full of football fanatics for good measure. In Wrexham I could go out with my family and almost get lost in the crowd. Occasionally I would be stopped and asked for my autograph etc., but in Manchester it seems impossible to go anywhere without being recognised.

Playing for Wrexham, if the team was doing poorly the crowd would give you some stick, but in Manchester it is quite different. There is more pressure on you playing for a club like United, and you are aware of the pressure because for one thing the crowds are much bigger.

The training with Manchester United is something new to me. Dave Sexton is clearly a very good coach with wide experience, and almost everything we do in training is done with the ball. At Wrexham it was sometimes hard graft, but I find I really enjoy the training with United.

Manchester United fans have acquired a bad name, but I haven't seen any signs of it. In my opinion the troublemakers represent only a very small percentage of the crowd, and these days you can in fact find troublemakers anywhere.

If you go into a pub for a quiet drink you frequently find there is a little bit of trouble that seems to be part of life these days. The difference is that trouble in small pubs doesn't get into the newspapers, while United fans causing trouble makes headlines, and is blown up out of all proportion.

When I first began playing at Old Trafford I found it very hard work. It was a big switch from the small crowds at Wrexham, and it is not easy to satisfy crowds of fifty thousand football crazy fans. But no doubt I'll get used to it.

*When Mike Thomas joined Manchester United he became friends immediately with Irish international Dave McCreery (photo above, left).*

*Wembley action above depicts the moment when Peter Shilton gave away the penalty that enabled Wales to beat England 1–0 in 1977*

I had already experienced some of the fanatical support at big matches when playing for Wales. Having dreamt of playing for Wales since I was about 14 I find the atmosphere and all the trappings just magic and the crowds at Welsh games are fantastic.

I have always looked forward to my games for Wales since my first cap in the Welsh FA's Centenary match against World Cup holders, West Germany. We lost 2–0, and if the Germans deserved to win with stars like Franz Beckenbauer and Berti Vogts, I thought we had chances and could have scored. Overall I thought we played quite well.

The best foreign team I have played against for Wales was Czechoslovakia when we lost 1–0 to them in a World Cup match in Prague. The Czechs that day had so many good players, with Antonin Panenka standing out above them all.

They were a really good side in Prague, but when we beat them 3–0 at Wrexham they were not even a shadow of that team. Clearly they do not relish playing in Britain, for they were so good in front of their own crowd.

I am often asked who are the key men in the Welsh side, and my stock answer is . . . 'all eleven'. Although we sometimes have a Third Division player in our team, everyone is aroused by a great feeling of patriotism and national fervour. Playing for Wales is something almost unique for the players.

To start with we have only a small population and not so many players to choose our team from, but everyone, whoever he is, goes out on the pitch to fight for Wales. In war, men die for their country, and some of that feeling seems to rub off on the players when they pull on a red shirt.

Obviously our manager Mike Smith, and coach Cyril Lea of Ipswich, must take a lot of credit for creating the right conditions in the Welsh camp. They are such good organisers, and are always full of interesting and helpful bits of information on the players of our opponents. Then again Mike Smith is a very good motivator. He winds you up, and makes you feel really great.

I was not yet in the side when Wales qualified for the quarter finals of the European Championship last time, but though we have some tough games to come I really do believe we can qualify again.

We hammered Malta 7–0, and beat Turkey 1–0, though that was a very hard fought game. The Turkish players were all very strong and physical which was a bit of a surprise to us. They were on our backs all the time and never let us play the way we can. Obviously it was a hard game as the score suggests.

But West Germany hold the key to our group. You have to respect the Germans for they have been really very good over the last few years and have lots of good players.

We drew 1–1 away to West Germany in December, 1977, and we gave full value for that result. I was down to play, but got injured in training the night before the game and had to drop out. But of course I saw the match and the red shirts did us proud. Another performance like that in the critical away game to Germany and we will be half way there. When we drew in Germany they had Sepp Maier and Vogts, as well as Rainer Bonhof and their high flying centre forward Klaus Fischer, but they only really played well for twenty five minutes while Wales kept up the pressure throughout.

Having seen that game I must be optimistic about the Germans but it is clear that the game away to Turkey will be a critical one too. But overall I feel we can do it.

For a while Wales missed the skill and speed of Leighton James who went through a bad patch. Not having many naturally gifted players to choose from we felt his absence. But he has settled down again at Burnley and he came back to help us win 1–0 against Turkey and did very well. At his best he can be a match winner, and the signs are that he has recovered his enthusiasm and best form.

If the future looks good with Wales I am equally confident about Manchester United developing into one of the top teams again. Last season we had a lot of injuries and found it difficult to turn out a settled side. But on paper United have a great team with Martin Buchan and Gordon McQueen supreme in defence, and a lot of good attacking players. All we need in my opinion is a couple of good results at the start of the season and we will take off.

For my part, I feel much more relaxed playing with good players around me. It is always easier to play with good players, and the United side is full of them.

So on both fronts I look forward to the near future with confidence, and with a great deal of hope, that I am sure is justified.

*'It is easy to play with good players and the United team is full of them' says Mike Thomas. One of the best is Martin Buchan shown in action on the right.*

adidas

# FOOTBALL IS BECOMING LESS WA

*says*

**Czech star**
**MARIAN MASNY**
**of Slovan Bratislava**

*Marian Masny, shown on the left, says the Czechs showed at Wembley last season that they are better in the air now. On the right, reserve centre back Ladislav Jurkemik wins a heading duel to underline this.*

# HANGING BUT INTERESTING TO CH

PLAYING for Czechoslovakia I have experienced more ups and downs than most players for though I think everyone will agree we were worthy winners of the European Championship in 1976, we failed completely in the 1978 World Cup qualifying campaign and played particularly poorly against Wales at Wrexham where we lost 3–0.

Our 1976 team was a very strong and experienced side that grew in understanding and confidence as it progressed with the passage of time. We were beaten 3–0 by England at Wembley in October, 1974, in our first European qualifying round match, but building on that side we then played 25 matches without a single defeat.

At that time we had two really outstanding players in goalkeeper Ivo Viktor and our *libero* Anton Ondrus who were both at the peak of their form in the period 1975 to 1976.

Ondrus and Jozef Capkovic formed a very strong central partnership in defence and we also had our captain at right back, Jan Pivarnik, playing very well too.

*Jan Pivarnik (below) the captain of the Czech team that won the 1976 European Championship is about to don a Scotland shirt after the Czechs had beaten Scotland 1–0 in Bratislava.*

The midfield block in that side was particularly strong. But that trio, Jaroslav Pollack, Antonin Panenka and Jozef Moder, are I think, past their best now.

In 1977 we lost goalkeeper Viktor through a back injury and had no really experienced substitute for him, and of course Anton Ondrus was suspended for three World Cup games, after being sent off with Andy Gray in Prague, when we beat Scotland 2–0. We missed them both badly, but this cannot disguise the fact that we played very poorly in 1977 and early 1978.

But today's team is improving a lot and in the autumn of 1978 we played very well, even though the team is in the process of being re-built. For a start we won 3–1 in Stockholm against Sweden in our first qualifying game for the 1980 European Championship, and then after beating Italy 3–0 in Bratislava, we played very well against England at Wembley, and were, I thought, a little unfortunate to be beaten 1–0.

*Photo above shows 1976 team manager Vaclav Jezek now in charge of Feyenoord, on the phone, and left, Anton Ondrus, the libero who played such a vital role in the 1976 success. He missed the Wembley game last season because he was injured in a car crash the previous week.*

Hopefully, I think we can do well in the near future, for the level of the game in Europe as a whole does not seem to me to be as high as it was in 1976, and we are improving again.

Over the last five years or so the best teams in Europe have been West Germany and Holland, and of course, as everyone knows, both sides have lost the services of their big personality players.

Holland have lost Johan Cruyff, and the Germans have had to play without key men like Gerd Müller and Franz Beckenbauer, and I think it shows in the play of both these teams.

By comparison with the performance of European teams in the 1978 World Cup, I think the standard of European football was higher in 1976. I say that, not just because Czechoslovakia did well, but because I really think the quality of football was better and the top teams had a more positive, attacking approach, and the matches were more exciting and dramatic.

Since then I think that only Italy have improved a little.

It is difficult for me to comment on the England team, for my only knowledge of them is based on the games in 1974 and 1978. The game five years ago was a competitive match while last year it was only a friendly, and I think that made a difference. I also think that our team of 1978 was much more experienced in playing against British teams than the 1974 side was.

In 1974 our team was subjected to a lot of pressure, but last time I was a little disappointed by the play of the English, and in particular by their attack. The forwards hardly created anything, and their play was stereotyped.

But as I have already said, it is difficult to compare—not least because we are more experienced against teams like England now, and we played harder in 1978, 'fighting' a lot more, and also much

improved in our heading.

No doubt the star of the England team was goalkeeper Peter Shilton who really saved England, for I think we should have scored, and won!

Then I also liked Dave Watson, and Steve Coppell (in the second half). But I must say I expected much more from Kevin Keegan who was disappointing because I had heard how well he was playing for Hamburg SV.

Perhaps the country I like to visit best is Spain, although generally it is said that we footballers only know the airports, the hotels and the stadiums. That is largely true of course, but I must say that what I have seen of Spain appeals to me.

I have visited Spain quite often, playing with Slovan Bratislava in summer tournaments in Barcelona, Huelva, Madrid and Gibraltar. I liked the general atmosphere and the games were not particularly defensive. Also the marking was not so tight—and that suits my style of play very well.

I was born on the 13th August, 1950, in a small village called Chynorany, near Topolcany. By the time I was sixteen I was playing in the highest junior league in Czechoslovakia for the nearby team of Banovce nad Bebravou.

By the time I was 18 I had reached their first team, and then, called up for military service I played in the Second Division for two seasons with Dukla Banska Bystrica, and in the summer of 1971 I was transferred to Slovan.

Strangely perhaps, my father was never interested in sport of any kind, but my elder brother Vojtech, twelve years older than me, was a very good player. He played for most of his career with the First Division team Jednota Trencin and then, after playing in Austria for two years with First Vienna FC, he retired to become a coach.

*One of the stars of the Czech team that won the European Championship in 1976 was Antonin Panenka, seen on the left, right arm raised after scoring against Russia. In the 1976 final against West Germany, Jan Svehlik (in action above) scored the vital first goal.*

Vojtech was an inside left and is now the assistant manager of Trencin. As a matter of interest the Czech name Vojtech is the equivalent of Bella in Hungarian, and my brother was usually referred to as Bella. Even more strangely, when I joined Slovan, the older players there began to call me Bella, and the nickname has stuck. No one ever calls me Marian.

I first played for Czechoslovakia in September, 1974. Our opponents were East Germany who had just done well in the World Cup and had a strong side with players like goalkeeper Jurgen Croy, Bernd Bransch, Hans-Jurgen Dorner and Joachim Streich. But we had a very good day in that match in Prague and we won 3–1. I think I had quite a good game, and I remember laying on the pass for Premysl Bicovsky to score the second goal. Anyway, after that I missed very few games for Czechoslovakia, and at the end of 1978 I had earned 45 full caps and scored 13 international goals.

With Slovan Bratislava we have a new coach, Anton Malatinsky, who came back after working in Holland, in the summer of 1978, and with him we work very hard at the game. Playing on Sundays, in a week where we have no extra game, we have a massage on Monday, and then train twice every day on Tuesday, Wednesday and Thursday. On Tuesday we usually do just physical work (running without a ball), and on Wednesday and Thursday, part of the training will be a practice match. On Friday, we train for about half an hour and we also do a little light training on Saturdays.

That programme was the way we started last autumn, but once the season got under way we had mid-week matches almost every week, so then we began to train just once a day for about 90 minutes.

One thing I do not like about being an international player is long training camps or long tours abroad. I think most of my colleagues feel the same way, unhappy to be away from our homes and families for very long.

In my opinion, three to five days in a training camp should be enough to rest, prepare, and concentrate on a match. Since Dr. Jozef Venglos took over the Czechoslovak team at the start of the 1978–79 season that has been his approach too, which suits me fine.

If we have a match on a Wednesday we usually meet on the previous Sunday, but for competitive games we spend five days in preparation, sometimes six.

The greatest success that I have experienced as a player, was of course, helping to win the European Championship in 1976. First we had to eliminate England in the qualifying round, and we beat them, a little fortunately I thought, 2–1 in Bratislava. That was a good day for me for I played quite well generally, and it was from my passes that both goals came. One was from a corner I took, aimed at the near post and Zdenek Nehoda got in to head the first goal, and I also beat a man before crossing for the winning goal, headed by Dusan Gallis.

Then we had to overcome the Soviet Union, never an easy task, and in the semi-final in Yugoslavia we beat Holland 3–1. In the final we were leading West Germany 2–0, but they got one back and scored an equaliser right on time. So we had to play extra time, and with no further score, we won on penalty kicks.

I played quite well in both games in Yugoslavia, and I think I did well at Wembley last autumn, particularly in the first half. Another match high in my list of happy memories was our 3–1 win over Sweden last year when I scored two goals and had a big hand in making the third for Nehoda.

As I have already said, it is difficult for me to judge England on just two games, four years apart, but as far as I can tell it seems to me that while English football has a great number of good players, they seem to lack the outstanding stars of the recent past like Bobby Moore.

England probably has more good players than any other country in Europe for they have always had clubs doing well in the European competitions. But super class players seem to be rare in England.

Liverpool of course are world famous, but many other English clubs have done well too in the European competitions. Generally, all the English players are fast, strong and skilful, and specially good at heading, but the English game has always seemed to me to be slightly stereo-typed, lacking I think the really top quality creative midfield players.

For all continental teams it is difficult to get a good result when playing in England, against clubs or the national team. The English fans really know how to support their teams and visiting sides are always subjected to very heavy pressure. Only the really good continental teams can do well against an English team *in England.*

Away from home, both England and English clubs are less of a problem for some reason. As far as I can remember the national team has never made any real impact on the game when playing away.

Scotland and Wales play a very similar style to England, perhaps because so many of their top players play in the English League. Like England they are much stronger at home than they are away.

Wales in my view are probably on a par with the average continental team while Scotland are a bit better than Wales generally. It is particularly difficult to beat Scotland at Hampden Park, and at home the Scots are among the best supported teams, and also among the roughest and toughest in my experience.

The best individual players of my playing career have been men like Franz Beckenbauer; Johan Cruyff and Kevin Keegan.

Beckenbauer was tremendously calm and cool under pressure, and had tremendous vision. Cruyff had really exceptional skill, and Keegan stands out I think, for the amount of work he gets through in both midfield and attack. But all three players understood how to use their special talents for the benefit of their team.

As a striking forward who tries to score goals as well as make them I have never enjoyed playing against Italian defenders. I cannot single out any one Italian, but they all seem to mark really tight, and they also use their hands and arms to hold you and obstruct you.

I like at least half a yard to play in, and you never get that from an Italian defender, which is I think why I never play specially well against them.

But the West German left back Bernard Dietz is also an unpleasant opponent and in particular I don't like to remember Danny McGrain of Scotland who treated me rather badly when we met at Hampden Park.

*Marian Masny thinks that Franz Beckenbauer, Johan Cruyff and Kevin Keegan have been the best players of his time, but he was disappointed with Keegan when he played against Czechoslovakia at Wembley last autumn. Keegan (number 7 below) is stopped here by goalkeeper Pavol Michalik with Ladislav Jurkimik (3) covering.*

Overall, world wide, I don't think that football is becoming any better, but it is *changing*, slowly. Defensive systems are getting better all the time and every year it becomes more difficult to score and make chances.

Football is progressively becoming faster, tougher, and more demanding for the players, but sometimes less attractive for the spectators. On the other hand we still see quite a few exciting games, full of drama.

It is difficult for me to judge whether the game is getting better really. In Czechoslovakia for example, the older generation of fans insist that the football of the thirties, played by Planicka, Bican and Nejedly was the most beautiful to watch.

But the middle age group seem to think that our team around 1960 was the best, with players like Masopust, Pluskal and Kvasnak standing out.

All I can say is that I hope that twenty years from now, some of the fans will say that the football played by Ondrus, Panenka, Nehoda, and perhaps .... Marian Masny was the best.

*Marian Masny (dark shirt) beats Bjorn Andersson of Sweden.*

# WEST BROMWICH FANS APPRECIATE GOOD FOOTBALL

*writes*

**JOHN WILE**

☆ ☆ ☆ ☆ ☆

I was born on the 9th March, 1947 in that hot bed of football, Sherburn, County Durham, and almost inevitably my first club was Sunderland.

When I was young I was quite small, and played at inside forward and switched to centre back one day when a player didn't turn up for a game. I was playing for Durham City in the Northern Premier League when I was 18, and a scout from Sunderland saw me and invited me to have a trial.

In the north-east I never really made a mark, though playing for Durham District Boys XI, I earned my only representative honour. After 18

*Tony Brown (photo above) sends the goalkeeper the wrong way to score from the spot at Ipswich, and, facing page, Laurie Cunningham in action for Young England.*

months with Sunderland they decided to let me go, and I moved to Peterborough United on a free transfer.

One game that does stand out in my memory during my Sunderland days was one in which I was asked to play centre forward—and scored a hat trick!

After spending three and a half years with Peterborough, I was transferred to West Brom, and it is really with them that I have made my mark and played my best football.

The West Bromwich fans are a really good crowd, probably one of the best in the country. They had some good sides in the 1950's but after that they hit a dull patch and were relegated to the Second Division.

The supporters have seen some lean times but since winning promotion West Brom have improved steadily, and the fans really appreciate good football.

In season 1977–78 I really thought we were going to make a mark on the game in the FA Cup. But in the semi-finals we came up against Ipswich Town and everything seemed to go wrong for us. It was the day I clashed heads with Brian Talbot and after playing for a while with my head bleeding, I had to go off for stitches in the wound.

It probably looked worse than it was, for it only needed three stitches. It was a peculiarly shaped cut, triangular in pattern, but I am sure that my injury didn't affect the outcome.

Every side gets a day like that when they just cannot get going and don't play up to their potential. So while we struggled to put our game together, Ipswich were playing very well and on the day they deserved to win.

*West Brom favourite Cyrille Regis in action (facing page) and photo right, John Wile goes off to have stitches in a head wound during the F.A. Cup semi-final with Ipswich in 1978. 'My injury didn't affect the result, it was just one of those days' he says.*

My game with West Brom is not really a tight marking job on the opposing centre forward. We prefer to cover space rather than mark men and my role is to go for the ball while my colleague Alistair Robertson does the sweeping up job.

This system works well for us, and I wouldn't like to see English sides playing the tight marking Italian game. To do that you have to mark all the opponents strikers and also their midfield men. That way you leave yourself short up front, and you can never get flowing, attacking football that way.

West Brom have had the potential to do well for some time. In fact we were already a very good side when our manager, Ron Atkinson took over. It could have been difficult for him, because we were already doing well, but wisely he didn't make any dramatic changes, but altered a few little things gradually and under his leadership we seemed to get a boost and really took off.

Mr. Atkinson's biggest asset is his ability in the field of man management. Of course it is necessary to have a deep knowledge of the game as well, but man management is vital. He has the knack of creating the right atmosphere and getting the best out of each player.

Another very important factor is Mr. Atkinson's obvious enthusiasm for the game, for this rubs off onto the players and acts as a further stimulant.

Last season we met some good foreign sides in the UEFA Cup, and I really thought we were going to have a lot of trouble with the Spanish club Valencia, who have the 1978 World Cup top scorer, Mario Kempes.

When I saw Kempes playing for Argentina on television he looked a really exciting player. He has a lot of skill and is a deadly finisher, and he is also strong enough to shrug off quite fierce tackles.

In the World Cup he showed his ability to beat a man, and then being quick, he had space in which to accelerate, gathering speed before the next defender could challenge him.

When we knew we were going to meet Valencia we discussed him and formed our own ideas about how to prevent him causing real trouble. Clearly he could be very dangerous if given the chance, but we decided not to mark him so tight and give close cover to the man that challenged him first. In that way we prevented him from using his speed to full advantage.

No doubt Kempes could punish sides that allowed him to play to his strengths, but in the two games we had with Valencia he didn't do too much.

The most impressive foreign side I have ever played against was Dynamo Tbilissi. We met them in Spain three years ago in a pre-season tournament, and though they arrived after 36 hours of travel due to delays, and almost went straight onto the pitch when they arrived, they played really excellent football.

I was much more impressed with them than most people were by Holland in the 1974 World Cup. I

*Ron Atkinson, photo above, has the knack of man-management, writes John Wile.*

*Argentinian World Cup star, Mario Kempes, photo right, who failed to impress against West Brom.*

thought that a lot of things the Dutch did were very basic. In some cases they were also very unprofessional, trying to play football in areas where it was not 'on', and sometimes they were very casual in their passing.

It often appears to me that the English tend to over-emphasise how much we can learn from the continentals, and hold them up too much. Certainly there are things we can learn from them, but we should not denigrate ourselves as some do.

There are things about the game to be learned from everyone, and the foreigners can learn a lot from us. In this game everyone can learn from each other.

The two players that take the eye at West Brom currently are of course our forwards, Cyrille Regis and Laurie Cunningham.

Regis has been a revelation, for he is strong, quick, and very good in the air. He is improving all the time too in his play on the ground and in my book he is the best centre forward in England.

One contributory reason for his success last season, was the fact that he was new to most defenders, an unknown quantity. Defenders generally don't yet have enough experience playing against him to learn how to try and counter his strengths.

Cunningham was clearly a good player when he joined us from Orient but in 1977–78 he had one or two injuries and couldn't get going. But last season he was a revelation. He has tremendous pace and like Kempes is able to take on people and cut up a defence. But though very much an individual he appreciates the players around him too.

Looking around the other top clubs I am often asked who are the most difficult strikers to handle, but this is a question too complicated for a straight answer.

The truth is that you can play against a big name player this week and have no problem, but the following week the same man could murder you. There are a lot of quality players about, but they all have off days, and specially good days too.

For myself, I spend quite a bit of time coaching football in schools. While playing myself, it is difficult to get too deeply involved because I can never see the teams that I coach, actually play. But football is what I know best and I would certainly like to stay in the game in some capacity, after my playing days are over.

So much for myself, and if I find it impossible to pick out star players to mention by name, obviously the big teams of the moment are Liverpool and Notts Forest, particularly as they played in 1977–78.

Forest are a bit like West Brom in that they have a lot of people that are not stars but are good players who play for each other, and the chemistry is right. They have a tremendous goalkeeper in Peter Shilton who is their biggest influence, and Tony Woodcock is very dangerous though he was not quite so outstanding last season. Forest are an excellent side with good players, a good manager, and a good set up.

But Liverpool in my opinion are in a class of their own. The way they played against us for the first 20 minutes last season was the best football I have ever seen anywhere. If Liverpool were ever to play that way for the full 90 minutes, no one could touch them.

*'Notts Forest are one of the big teams of the moment' says John Wile, and Peter Shilton in action below, 'is their biggest influence'.*

# DUTCH CLUBS WOULD LIKE SOME ENGLISH PLAYERS

*says*

**ARNOLD MÜHREN**

of Ipswich Town and Holland

IN many ways I have followed in the footsteps of my elder brother Gerrie.

I was born in Veendam, a small town north of Amsterdam on the 2nd of June, 1951, and like Gerrie I first played for our local team, Volendam, and then moved on to Ajax.

Like Gerrie too I emigrated to further my football career, for he is now playing in Spain and of course we are both midfield players.

When I was 19 years old I moved to Ajax after Rinus Michels had watched me play for Volendam and invited me to join the Amsterdam club. But soon after that Michels went off to Barcelona, and when I actually joined Ajax the new manager-coach was the Rumanian Stefan Kovacs.

I stayed with Ajax for three and a half happy years but unfortunately I did not play in any of the European Cup Finals. I did play in quite a few European Cup games, including both legs of a semi-final with Real Madrid when we drew 1–1 at home, and then won 1–0 in Madrid, and I also played in the semi-finals against Bayern Munich away. But Ajax at that time had a midfield trio that was outstanding: Johan Neeskens, Arie Haan, and my brother Gerrie.

So I was only a reserve, playing about 20 games a year when someone was injured.

At that time of course Ajax were a super team, winning everything, so I had no cause to complain.

At international level I played six times for Holland's Under 23 team and also played for the full side when they beat Tunisia by 3–0. I also played for the Dutch representative team that met a team of foreigners playing in Holland, but that has been the limit of my international experience so far.

When I first began playing for Ajax they were unbelievably good, feted all over Europe, and of course the key player was Johan Cruyff.

*Arnold Mühren in action (facing page) for Ipswich Town, and, on the left, his new team-mate George Burley.*

adidas

The Dutch game was very skilful generally at that time, and everyone admired them when the best Dutch players got together to provide some unforgettable football in the 1974 World Cup.

Now unfortunately, all the big stars have left Holland and the game there has declined. Now the Dutch fans are being offered what I call 'work' football, lacking the magic it once had.

Football in Holland today is much slower than the English game, being more like chess. The build up towards goal is very slow, and compared to the

*Ipswich favourite Paul Mariner in action (facing page) and above Arnold Mühren greets his former FC Twente clubmate Frans Thijssen when he signed for Ipswich.*

English style, many more players are involved in each attack, carefully trying to pass the ball from one end of the pitch to the other.

The typically English game has more *tempo*, played at a higher rhythm and with more long passes. So in England, the build up towards goal is much faster, and there are many exciting incidents in front of goal which I think the spectators like.

Dutch fans would like to see something from English football I am sure, because they would enjoy the thrills and excitement. Probably both England and Holland would benefit if they adapted their game and learned a little bit from each other.

English football is generally more exciting and all the games are fiercely competitive. With Ipswich you cannot be sure of winning, even at home to the team at the bottom of the First Division. But in Holland there are the big clubs like Ajax, PSV Eindhoven and Feyenoord, joined sometimes, and only temporarily, by one or two other clubs who happen to have good players, and they are always at the top. The other clubs simply have no chance against the giants in Holland because the big clubs sign up all the best players.

English football may be a little tougher, and every game is physically hard and demanding, though the standard of refereeing is probably about the same.

There are not so many really big personalities in English football, no one to compare with the best players I have ever seen like Johan Cruyff and Mario Kempes, Argentina's centre forward in the last World Cup. But the general level is very high.

It is this very high average level of ability that makes the English championship the best in the world, and the best English club in my opinion is Liverpool. They seem to have learned lots of things from their many experiences in European competition, and while they retain the same individual characteristics of the English players, their style of play is a bit more like continental football.

*Mick Mills the Ipswich captain who has been an England regular for some time.*

I was the first Dutch player to move to England but it seems very likely that I will be followed by one or two more quite soon. I know that quite a few English managers are looking at Dutch players. Yet strangely enough, even the top Dutch clubs like Ajax would like to have one or two English players.

Ajax have one now in centre forward Ray Clarke. They like English players because they are probably the best in the world at heading and they work right through the ninety minutes.

I have found that living in England is not so different from life in Holland. The Ipswich manager and coach, Bobby Robson and Cyril Lea, as well as all the players, have gone out of their way to be kind and helpful and to make me feel at home.

Even the people I meet in the town, and in the shops etc., are not unlike Dutch people.

English food has a bad reputation on the continent, but I have found it to be very good and almost the same as in Holland. And the cost of living in England is much lower. Cars and food for example are much cheaper in England than they are in Holland.

No doubt it was a big help to me that I already spoke English when I joined Ipswich. Both my brother Gerrie and I studied English in school and kept it up.

The language is no problem to my family either, for neither of my two children are yet old enough to go to school, and by the time they are five they should speak English very well.

My son Aryan is two and a half years old and already goes quite happily to a play school, while my daughter Claudia who is only one, will grow up speaking English quite naturally.

I was very glad to join Ipswich and play in English football for I think that to most professional players in any country, to make it at top level in England is to prove yourself.

Four years ago I was transferred from Ajax to FC Twente in an exchange deal. Ajax fancied the Twente midfield player Rene Notten, who looked like becoming a big star, and I moved to Twente in a straight swap.

FC Twente are a club that does very well usually, managing to hang on to a position about 5th or 6th in most recent seasons, and always giving the big clubs a very hard game. But Twente play in a small town near the German border called Enschede, and as a small town team they only manage to pull in attendances of around 9,000 to 10,000.

*Ipswich manager Bobby Robson who very shrewdly stepped into the Dutch market before transfer fees exploded in England.*

FC Twente have had a lot of good players in recent years, including the Van der Kerkhoff twins who played for Holland in the World Cup Final in Argentina. But they transferred them to PSV.

Every year it is the same for FC Twente. They have to sell at least one player for a big transfer fee, to balance their books. If they did not, then they would go bankrupt, so that when Ipswich made a tempting offer for me they had to let me go, and I have no regrets at all that I came to play in England.

All I want to do is to play well and help Ipswich win one of the major honours.

# PLAYING FOR LIVERPOOL HAS BEEN A DREAM FOR ME

says
PHIL NEAL
of Liverpool and England

SOME of my Liverpool colleagues have been at the club throughout their careers and have been brought up on success, but I think that perhaps I appreciate the good things that have come my way more than most.

You see, before joining Liverpool I had seven years playing with Northampton Town and in my time with them, the club had to apply for re-election twice!

From that background, joining Liverpool and earning almost every honour in the game during four years with Liverpool was like a fairy story.

Born in a little Northamptonshire village called Irchester on the 20th of February, 1951, I began playing organised football at school when I was seven years old. At school I always played up front, and naturally, scoring goals was the name of the game.

My father played football, just as an amateur—

*'Northampton were the only club to retain their interest in me after I decided to stay on at school for "O" Levels'*

what used to be called an inside forward—so I suppose football was in my blood, even if I did live off the main soccer highway.

During my schooldays I played for the school team and a local Boys' Club, and later my whole week end was devoted to the game when I played for Wellingborough Schools team on Saturday morning, and played for a Sunday side twice, morning and afternoon.

I was fortunate to be chosen to play for Northamptonshire Schoolboys team and got through several trials for the England boys team. I was included in the final forty, but never made the team.

*Liverpool's Ray Kennedy in action (facing page), and above Ray Clemence goes down to save at the feet of West Ham's David Cross.*

At that time Tottenham offered to sign me as an apprentice, and I had a trial for West Brom. I visited a lot of clubs that showed interest in me but I decided to accept the advice of my schoolteacher and my parents, and stay on at school. They all wanted me to study and get 'O' Levels behind me in case I failed to make a living at the game.

The only club that maintained their interest in me was Northampton, so I signed for them when I left school, and was very fortunate to find myself playing for manager Ron Flowers, the former Wolves and England player. He firmly believed in bringing on young players and blooded a lot of youngsters. So it was that I played for Northampton, away to Walsall when I was 17, and winning 1–0, that's a red letter day in my mind.

Northampton being a struggling little club were always short of players, and I got shuffled around quite often. When a first team player was unfit, I filled in, even playing in attack, and at one stage I scored 8 goals in 9 games for Northampton. I even played in goal one day when the goalkeeper got injured.

Looking back I can appreciate now that experience in different positions was good for my development, and then, when I was 23, life suddenly changed for me.

Northampton had a good spell under manager Bill Dodgin, and we were more successful than for several seasons. I suppose this attracted the scouts, and finally I was transfered to Liverpool, as Bob Paisley's first signing after he took over from Bill Shankly.

With Liverpool I made my debut in the big local derby against Everton, though it was kept from me at the time until the last minute. That day I was expecting to play for the Reserves but on the morning of the match I was told to report to Goodison Park because Alec Lindsay was doubtful.

I remember walking across a park to Goodison with my boots tucked under my arm, thinking that there was no chance of playing, and that I was asked to go there just as cover, in case. But when I got there, I was told 'get changed, you are playing'.

We drew 0–0, and I suppose I must have done fairly well, because although I was left out of the side the following week, I got back in again very soon afterwards and settled down to become a regular first team choice.

Although I've scored a few goals now, the first one sticks in my mind. It was in an UEFA Cup match at home to the Spanish club, Real Sociedad of San Sebastian.

Since then, everything has gone like a dream for me. I played at Wembley for England and Liverpool, scoring the only England goal when we beat Northern Ireland 1–0 there. In my first three and a half years as a Liverpool player I have done almost everything, helping to win the European Cup twice; the UEFA Cup and the European Super Cup.

For England I first played in Don Revie's time, being chosen for the Centenary game of the Welsh FA at Wrexham in 1976, and again I was on the winning side. Later I scored one of my most memorable goals for England when we won 4–3 away to Denmark in a match that counted for the 1980 European Championship.

I remember that goal well, for it was a dream. I won the ball in a tackle and ran with it, and then from about eighteen yards I let fly and it went like a bomb into the roof of the net. Really, a big thrill.

Of course I have scored most of my goals from the penalty spot. I first started taking penalties for Northampton, but at Liverpool, Kevin Keegan used to take the spot kicks. Then one day Kevin missed one, and said he didn't want the job any more and I volunteered and got the job.

For three years I took penalties, scoring from a high percentage, until I missed a vital one.

Taking penalty kicks is not a special art, but a matter of confidence in your own ability, and having the right temperament for it. But playing for Liverpool, who are often on television, it was only a matter of time before goalkeepers began to anticipate where I was going to place my shot.

I know that Ray Clemence makes a point of watching all penalties on TV, studying how the players run up to the spot and which side they prefer to shoot.

So it seems natural that all other goalkeepers will do the same and they get to know your style too well. So it is just a matter of time before you begin to miss them, and that is it for a while.

My most important penalty was the one in the European Cup Final in Rome against Borussia Mönchengladbach, and I remember it well. We were leading 2-1 at the time, but the match was still wide

*Phil Neal has scored quite a lot of goals, many of them from the penalty spot. Above, he slots home a spot-kick for England against Hungary at Wembley.*

open, making it doubly important.

The Borussia goalkeeper was a giant, about six foot seven, and probably the biggest goalkeeper I have ever played against. He looked massive, almost filling the whole goal. But I scored and we went on to win so it worked out well.

Mönchengladbach are the best foreign team I have ever played against. The thing I admired most about them was their ability to play top drawer football so quickly. They could break out of defence and played with so much skill and speed. They moved from one end of the pitch to the other so fast. This was the hallmark of a very good side, for they made progress at speed because they played a lot of one-two's and even one touch football, and they threatened to score every time they got the ball at their own end.

Another outstanding foreign side was FC Barcelona who had the two big Dutch stars Cruyff and Neeskens at the time. Barcelona's stadium is probably the most impressive ground I have ever played on, and in a tremendous atmosphere we won 1–0. But underlining just how good a side they were, we could only draw against them, 1–1 at home in Liverpool.

Last season, having won the European Cup in two successive seasons, most people expected us to win it again and equal the records of Ajax and FC Bayern Munich, but it all went wrong against Notts Forest in the first round.

We were fairly confident that we could eliminate Forest and played in our usual attacking style. But they beat us in the first leg when they were at home and the tie was settled there. Forest sat back, content to contain us and hit us on the break. We learned a lot from that, and later when we met them in the league we beat them 2–0 by changing our play. We had learned not to go at them, and our win brought to an end their sequence of being unbeaten for more than a year.

*Liverpool and Scotland striker Kenny Dalglish (below) who is so often the key man in attack for club and country*

I am often asked who are the key men in the Liverpool side and if I mention Kenny Dalglish and Ray Clemence, I do so very reluctantly because at Liverpool it is so much a team effort. As England manager Ron Greenwood says he wants England to play, we keep it simple and play as a team, helping each other out all the time, and specially if someone is not having too good a game.

It seems to me that much of Liverpool's success stems from some very shrewd signings. All their players seem to want success and are willing to work hard for it, and this keeps the will to win going, even from one generation of players to another.

All the Liverpool players are geared to attack, which is what the game is about and everyone tries to get things right. I was probably a typically Liverpool signing, for I had never known any real success until I joined them.

Perhaps the fact that we really do just take every game as it comes, and set out to win it, is fundamental. Before a semi-final I have no thoughts of being at Wembley if we win. I just get myself into the right frame of mind to concentrate on todays' game and win, and I feel the other players do that too.

Rather than pick out individual Liverpool players I would prefer to single out Tommy Hutchison of Coventry City as a very good and dangerous player. He is under-rated in many quarters I am sure, because he doesn't get many goals himself. But he has a lot of skill, and long gangly legs that are deceptive, and he possesses a variety of tremendous body swerves that can send you the wrong way. You just have to stop him because he will murder you if you let him play, and he lays on so many chances for his colleagues.

Overall, England's future looks very bright to me for we have a successful full team again under Ron Greenwood, and a lot of very good players in our equally successful 'B' team and Under 21 side.

*Tommy Hutchison (photo above) 'will murder you, if you let him play' says Phil Neal.*

England have improved unbelievably since Ron Greenwood took over. He instilled confidence in everyone right from the start, and is the most knowledgeable person about the game that I have ever spoken to. He seems to know hundreds of little things that are very important when you add them all up, and he obviously has a thorough knowledge of world football.

Usually we meet for just three days before a game but it makes a nice break to meet different faces at training and the old enthusiasm quickly comes back. Mr. Greenwood has never asked me to change, or adapt my style of play, and I am sure he chooses his players based on what he sees them do for their clubs and simply picks a team that he thinks will be able to play well together.

All Ron Greenwood seems to want is that you reproduce your club form, and apart from my ambitions with Liverpool, I very much hope that I can go on and be part of the England set-up, for I am sure they will be successful and do very well in the 1980 European Championship.

# AS THE LEADING LEAGUE SCORER IN EUROPE, BARCELONA SIGNED ME TO GET GOALS IN SPAIN

**'My happiest memory of 1978 was my second goal in the World Cup game against West Germany to give Austria a 3–2 win over our neighbours—our first victory over them for 47 years'**

UP to the moment I moved to Barcelona I was a hundred-per-cent Vienna boy. I was born there, educated there, and the only club I played for right from the start was SC Rapid Vienna—though they did loan me to WAC for a while. I worked my way through the Rapid youth teams, and until 1972 I was a part-time footballer, working as a car mechanic during the day and training during the evenings. My father wasn't at all happy about the idea of me being a professional footballer though, and kept telling me to concentrate on a more secure career. But I think he's changed his mind now.

My development as a player is entirely due to the great treatment and advice I had at Rapid. Their youth-team trainer Sepp Pecanka was the man who had the greatest influence on me, I think. He helped

me to improve not only the technical aspects of the game, but also my whole mental approach to the profession I had chosen.

I know that winning the Golden Boot award as the top European goal scorer in league football in 1977–78 really lifted me to fame here and the World Cup gave me another big boost in terms of publicity. But I've been scoring goals in Austria for a long time now, and I've been top scorer every year since 1974. In fact I was runner-up for the Golden Boot in 1975, but few people remember the man who comes second.

People often ask me what the secret of my goalscoring is, but really I'm just the specialist who puts the ball in the net. I'm lucky to have a flair for scoring goals, but basically goals are a team effort.

If I had to single out anyone who perhaps helped me more than anyone else, it would be Herbert Prohaska who plays for FK Austria (Wien) and works wonders in midfield for the national team.

Talking about the national team, it was probably Austria's recent successes that brought my name to the fore on the international scene.

We've had a poor international record over the last twenty years, but the whole organisation of club football has been revised in recent years, and the standard of play has risen. So when the World Cup qualifying rounds came round, we were determined to qualify for Argentina. Most people thought that East Germany would have few problems in qualifying from our group, though obviously Austria were going to give them more headaches than Turkey or Malta.

We were the underdogs, and that was good for us. We knew that we should take four points from Malta without too much trouble, but Turkey are one of those middle-of-the-road teams who can spring surprises, and we knew that our results against them could be decisive.

In Vienna we overran Turkey, but they were difficult to break down in defence and we only scored once. And in the return match in Izmir we had to face a crowd of 85,000 fanatical Turkish supporters!

We didn't play at all well in Turkey but we got the result that we wanted—a 1–0 win that guaranteed our trip to Argentina.

Our hunch about the Turks was correct, though, because in the meantime they had surprised everyone by drawing 1–1 away to the East Germans, and it was this point that eventually decided the group in our favour.

We shared the points with East Germany with two 1–1 draws, but those games aren't exactly a happy memory for me.

In the first match in Vienna the score was 1–1 with five minutes to go when I headed what was—I promise you—a perfectly good goal. I couldn't believe it when the referee disallowed it. He had already presented the East Germans with their equaliser by punishing our 'keeper for carrying the ball more than four steps. The indirect free kick was only a few yards from our goal and they scored from it. Anyway, I rushed up to the referee to protest. He was Mr. Tom Reynolds from Wales and I don't speak enough English to insult him or anything like that, but he sent me off for arguing.

I wept in the dressing-room because it was all a terrible injustice. I *knew* the goal was good. And at that stage it looked as though the dropped home point could mean the difference between qualifying for Argentina and staying at home. On top of that, I knew that the sending-off would mean that I'd automatically be suspended for the return match in East Germany. That was the blackest night of my career.

*Hans Krankl's high and low points in the 1978 World Cup qualifying campaign. Above, left, 'little' Malta whom Krankl hit for six goals in a 9–0 win, and right, referee Tom Reynolds who sent him off in the 1–1 draw with East Germany.*

In spite of the injustice, East Germany were definitely the best team in our group. They were superbly fit and very well drilled. It's difficult to single out individuals in Eastern European sides, because they tend to be good, solid teams with no 'star' players. Still, I think we thoroughly deserved to qualify because we matched them in all departments and had that little bit more skill and flair.

Argentina was a tremendous experience for me. People sometimes ask me what my happiest memories are, and most of them are concentrated into an incredible 1977–78 season. Six goals in our 9–0 win against Malta; seven goals for Rapid against Graz AK; the 41 league goals that won me the Golden Boot; the World Cup; my transfer to Barcelona . . . . it all happened so quickly.

We approached the World Cup finals with the same attitude as in the qualifying group. Few people tipped us to qualify from Group 3. We ourselves thought that Brazil might be a bit of a handful, but we thought we had a good chance of getting results against Spain and Sweden.

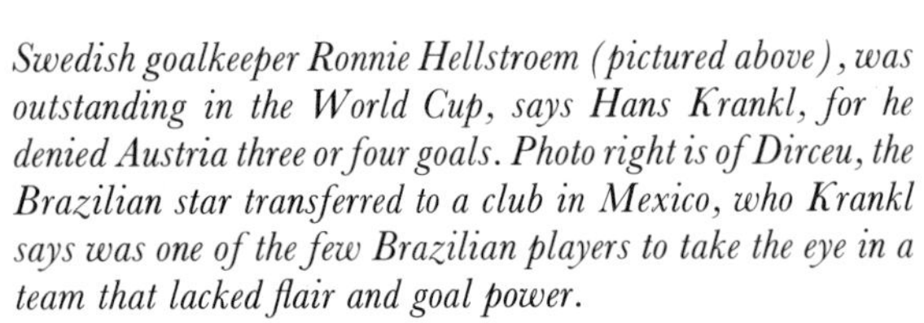

*Swedish goalkeeper Ronnie Hellstroem (pictured above), was outstanding in the World Cup, says Hans Krankl, for he denied Austria three or four goals. Photo right is of Dirceu, the Brazilian star transferred to a club in Mexico, who Krankl says was one of the few Brazilian players to take the eye in a team that lacked flair and goal power.*

We got off to a good start against Spain in our opening match. We admitted that they would probably have the edge on us in terms of individual ball skills, but we reckoned we could beat them on aggression, speed and team effort. And that's what happened really. We unsettled them and didn't give them time to play the game at their normal pace. I was very happy to score our winning goal.

So, we were very confident before the game against Sweden. I know we only won 1–0, and that was a goal I scored from the penalty spot, but we were always in command, I thought. Their goalkeeper Ronnie Hellstroem was outstanding, otherwise we could have won by three or four goals.

By the time we came to play Brazil we were already sure of a place in the last eight, and maybe that took a little of the competitive edge off our performance. Anyway, we didn't play very well.

Perhaps Brazilian teams of the past would have thrashed us, but the current team was definitely nothing very special. Dirceu and Mendonca caught the eye, but generally they seemed to lack flair and goalpower.

I think most people were disappointed with the Brazilians, and if the result had been more important for us—who knows? Perhaps we could have beaten them!

In the second round our morale faltered a bit. Psychologically we felt that, by reaching the last eight, we had already done all that could be expected of us, and I think this affected our performance.

That 5–1 defeat against Holland was certainly our worst game of the tournament. It was terrible. The Dutchmen scored early on, and we had to open up and look for goals, and that gave them the space they needed for their counter-attacks. I thought Jan Poortvliet played well, and Robbie Rensenbrink is always good when his side is on top.

*The action shot on the right is of Robbie Rensenbrink, the left winger of Anderlecht and Holland, who, says Krankl is always good when his side are on top.*

We didn't expect to win the next match against Italy, but, looking back, perhaps we could have done. In fact we *should* have done. We played much better than the Italians and if the referee had been better we would never have lost. Still, I mustn't say any more about that.

My happiest memory is our final match against West Germany, when we beat the 1974 champions 3–2. It was the first time Austria had beaten West Germany in 47 years, and I was very happy to score two of our three goals, particularly our winner just before the end. That was probably my favourite goal of all time.

A lot of people in Europe have said that Argentina didn't really deserve to win the World Cup, but I don't agree. Although we didn't play them, I thought they were the most positive attacking team in the tournament, and I particularly admired Leopoldo Luque and Mario Kempes.

For me, life certainly didn't quieten down after the World Cup—it got more hectic!

Within weeks I was in Barcelona to face an exciting new challenge. At first everything was very strange. I didn't speak any Spanish and had to rely on Johan Neeskens to translate everything for me. I found that hundreds of fans turn up to watch every training session, and there are always hordes of journalists around.

On a couple of occasions the press has twisted things I have tried to say in Spanish, so now I've decided not to give interviews for a while until I speak better Spanish.

Club football in Spain is very competitive, and the fans of clubs like CF Barcelona expect their team to win every match. The thing I find most different is that we have crowds of 80,000 for every home match, whereas in Vienna we rarely had more than 8,000!

So the atmosphere is terrific and certainly motivates the players.

Another big difference is that when the more modest clubs come to play in Barcelona they only try to defend—and they don't care how they do it.

Some of the tackling is very fierce, and I don't understand how anyone can deliberately set out to injure a fellow professional.

People warned me that Spanish referees were . . . . different, and that they always favour the home team. But I've few complaints so far. A lot of international class players are in Spain at the moment, and it's always interesting to play against top-class opposition.

*Argentina's World Cup centre forward, Leopoldo Luque, who impressed Hans Krankl in the big event of 1978*

I think the general standard of club football in Spain is quite high at the moment, though it's difficult to say where the best football is being played. Maybe the English and West German leagues are the most competitive, judging by their consistency in European Competitions—but it's difficult to judge without having played there.

Elsewhere there tends to be a handful of top clubs with the others a long way behind. But in recent years, clubs from unfashionable countries like France, Austria and Switzerland have had good international results, and I think there's been a general levelling-out of standards throughout Europe.

# SIGNING *ARDILES* AND *VILLA* WAS A GREAT MOVE FOR TOTTENHAM

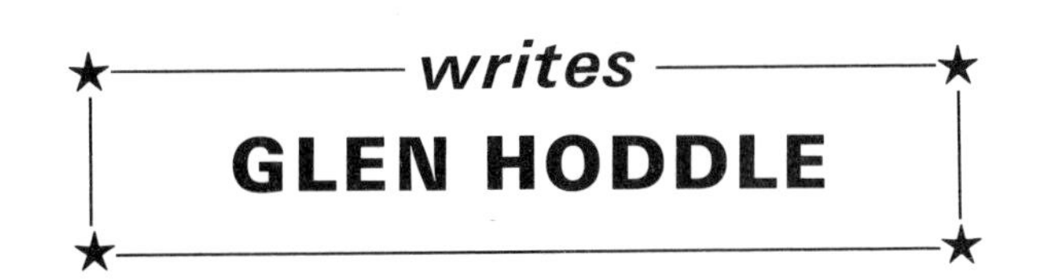

ALTHOUGH Tottenham Hotspur were relegated two years ago, the supporters at White Hart Lane have been really fantastic. Obviously it helped a lot that we bounced straight back up into the First Division, proving that we really belonged in the top class, but our attendances in the Second Division were better than most First Division sides.

It's hard to explain why we ever got relegated in the first place. I cannot put my finger on any reason. All I can think is that it is one of those things that happens to the best sides every now and again. It happened to Manchester United too of course, and who can say that ten years from now, despite all their success, that it will not befall Liverpool.

Of course there are some Spurs supporters who, living in the past, and brought up on the double-winning team, were unhappy watching Second Division football. But I would say that at least 80% of our fans remained extremely loyal.

The crowd at White Hart Lane have been specially good to me and I really appreciate it. Usually, professional players are too engrossed in the game to pay much attention to the crowd, but when the fans keep chanting your name, as they did with me, you just cannot fail to notice it. And it acts as a tremendous source of inspiration to me, boosting my confidence no end. And of course it is very flattering.

Unfortunately I found myself out of the team quite often last season, and not surprisingly, I was very disappointed. I even went so far as to ask for a transfer, but I honestly never wanted to leave Tottenham for I have always been very happy there, and it is the only club I have known. But every player wants first team football, and if it turns out that the only way I can get it is to leave, then that is what I will have to do, though I will be sorry to do it.

After being relegated, the players responded really well to the challenge of getting back into the First Division and I really enjoyed our promotion year. Probably it has been the high point of my career so far, to get back up first time.

*Osvaldo Ardiles (facing page) a big favourite with the fans, and left Ricardo Villa*

But then of course Tottenham signed the two Argentinians, Osvaldo Ardiles and Ricardo Villa, and it seemed to me unfortunate that I was the one who had to make room for them.

Let me make it clear that I think signing two World Cup stars was a great move by the club. They signed three year contracts, and if Tottenham can win something with them, as I believe they could, it would be a great boost and pacify the few fans that compare the present team unfavourably with the Danny Blanchflower–Jimmy Greaves team they loved so much.

With Ardiles playing really superbly, the crowds at Tottenham were even bigger than in our promotion year, and everywhere Spurs played last season, the fans came to see the two Argentinians. So obviously it was not only good for the club, but also good for the game as a whole.

The two Argentinians are quite different players in style. 'Ossie' is nicely balanced, being rather small, and extremely skilful, an outstanding player. But many people have in my opinion, been unfairly critical of Ricardo. He looks more cumbersome, and some seem to think he is a defensive player. But he is in fact very skilful and is really an attacking player too.

So signing the two Argentinians must be viewed as a good thing for Spurs but I still have the feeling that there are many young players in England who could become just as good and I don't think English clubs should go overboard chasing foreigners.

Many foreign players that I have seen are in fact very ordinary, and many of them wouldn't live in the cut and thrust of English league football over 42 games. What the clubs must do is be very selective, and only bring over the really top grade stars.

To underline the strength of English football, I really believe that the best team I have ever seen or played against was Liverpool last season. When they beat us 7–0 at Anfield early last season they were unbelievably good, really at their peak. Many of their players played out of their skins that day, and no one could have touched them on that performance.

*John Pratt in action (left) who coached Glen Hoddle as a boy, and (facing page), another Spurs favourite Peter Taylor.*

I have been at Tottenham since I was eleven years old, training with them on Tuesday and Thursday evenings—under my present colleague John Pratt, surprisingly. He used to supervise our training, and Pat Welton used to come and watch when we played training games.

Then when I was sixteen I signed as an apprentice professional, and a year later I was a full time professional.

The English newspapermen seemed to take to me immediately, and said some very kind things about me being skilful. But looking back I don't think that I had to work specially hard at my skills when I was young.

My father played as an amateur for several top clubs like Hayes and Uxbridge, so perhaps football is in my blood. He told me that when I was only ten months old, my mother threw a ball to me, and while they expected me to pick it up and throw it back—I kicked it!

As a boy I played in scratch games as often as I could, playing every hour of every day that I had free. I was certainly very keen, but I just seemed to develop naturally.

Of course I know about my weaknesses though, and I work at them very hard in training. It is widely known that I am at my best going forward, but if I never experienced any problems in that department I know that my defensive qualities leave something to be desired.

I keep this constantly in mind when I play in training games. The part of the game that comes naturally to me, in attack, I just let happen when I get the ball, but I consciously tell myself throughout the game that I must make a special effort to help win the ball back when my team loses possession. With this in mind, and hoping that constant practice will improve my defensive qualities I work really hard at it.

Most other players know their weaknesses too, but it seems to me that one of the problems in English football is that many good defensive players do not work to improve their attacking skills and practice to achieve mastery of the ball. That seems to me to be criminal.

On the continent the players train in the afternoons to improve their skills and I really believe that English players should do that too, with obvious advantages to the individuals and to the game

generally. But for some reason it just doesn't happen in England.

Some people feel that English football is too fast and too hard to allow really skilful players to develop here and they cite the Dutch star Johan Cruyff as an example.

In my opinion they play a different game on the continent but the best English players are just as skilful. The biggest difference is that abroad they play at a slower pace and thus the continental players have more time on the ball to reproduce their skills. English players have to produce their skill in much tighter areas and at a higher level of pace. If we were to drop our pace I am sure that very many English players would be seen to be just as skilful as the top class foreigners.

You get more knocks and injuries in England if you have a lot of skill, but I haven't found very many players who foul me deliberately. It is just that a player who holds the ball near the opponents goal over ninety minutes will inevitably get involved in late tackles.

But if I don't really want to knock our referees they could improve a bit I think. Over the last three years the match officials seemed to me to be getting a better grip on the game. But last season it seemed to me that they let things slip back a bit by concentrating too much on the wrong things like bad language, handling, and throwing the ball away when free kicks are given. That type of thing.

Whatever the critics might say about the pace of the English game I think George Best proved that the players with real class can still develop here. George was the best player I ever saw, better even than Cruyff and Pelé. I rated him so highly because he was a complete footballer, and as an individual he could often win a game, or earn a point on his own by producing a little bit of magic. He could tackle and head the ball as well as most and I really believe that he could have played well in any position, even at full back or centre half.

Personally, I prefer to play in midfield but I think I benefitted from having some games up front last season. Playing in a fully attacking role gave me an insight into the kind of service the strikers really need, and I hadn't fully appreciated that before I played there myself. So although I was not too keen to play up front, I certainly benefitted from it, for it can only improve my game.

I was very fortunate to get off to an early start in league football, for Tottenham manager Terry Neil gave me my first game away to Stoke City when I was only 17. We won 2–1 that day, and I was lucky enough to score the winning goal and kept my place. After that I was a regular first teamer for three seasons, until my problems began last season.

But all I really want now is first team football and the opportunity to develop into a better all round player. Hopefully too, I would like to play for England, having played for the England Youth team when they won the 'little World Cup' in Switzerland, when we beat Finland 1–0 in the final. And later I was fortunate enough to play several times in a successful England Under 21 side.

But I can only do that playing first team football, and though I realise that no one can be guaranteed a regular first team place, if in the end I feel I will have a better chance somewhere else, then I will very reluctantly have to leave Tottenham.

*George Best, in action (facing page) is proof that British players can still develop their skills in English football, says Glen Hoddle, 'Better than Cruyff and Pelé' he says. He believes English clubs should try to improve their players skills. Below, Spurs captain Steve Perryman.*

*Cruyff captains Ajax for the last time (above with Sepp Maier) against Bayern München. Below he guests for New York Cosmos, and (facing page) fouled even in his farewell friendly on 7th November, 1978 in Amsterdam.*

# ★★★★★★★★ I.F.B. SALUTES JOHAN CRUYFF ★★★★★★★★

*Johan Cruyff first played for Ajax in 1964, starting as a goal-scoring centre forward. For Ajax he spearheaded their attack that won the league championship six times and the Dutch FA Cup four times.*

*Season 1966–1967 was his most successful for he was the highest scorer in the Ere-Divisie with 33 goals, while Ajax did the Cup and League double.*

*With Ajax, Cruyff helped to win the European Cup three times in 1971, 1972, and 1973. The finals of 1971 and 1973 were poor matches, but the 1972 final against FC Internazionale in Rotterdam was a fine game in which Cruyff scored both goals in a 2–0 win. Three times Cruyff was voted 'European Footballer of the Year' in 1971, 1973, and 1974.*

*In 1973 Cruyff was transferred to C. F. Barcelona and with them he helped win the championship in 1974 and the Cup in 1978. Cruyff underlined his all round ability by becoming a general rather than a striker, and thus in his last 4 seasons in Spain he scored only 31 goals. Probably the most skilful player of his time, he was certainly the most popular.*

# MY STRENGTH IS

*Gary Owen (above) and right, in action with Dave Clement of Q.P.R.*

# IN GOING FORWARD

*writes*

**GARY OWEN**

**of Manchester City**

TO outsiders it may appear that Manchester City suffer in the shadow of Manchester United, but if this might have been true at one time, it is not true today. For example, in season 1977–78, the attendances at Maine Road were not much below those of United, and when we start to play well I am sure they will go even higher.

What made the difference to City and their supporters was the successful period from about 1966 when, under the guidance of Joe Mercer and Malcolm Allison, City won the FA Cup and the League, and also the European Cupwinners Cup.

In my time, City have twice qualified for the UEFA Cup and of course, finished as runners up in the League, one point behind Liverpool. So, bearing in mind that Manchester United were relegated once, our record over the last ten years compares very favourably.

I was very pleased when Malcom Allison re-joined the club as coach last season for I was greatly impressed by him in his first spell with the club, even though I was only a schoolboy at the time.

Gary Owen was a nobody at that time, but I remember that he went out of his way to talk to me, and asked me about my weaknesses etc. Then he took me out on the training pitch alone for half an hour, even though I was so young. This really impressed me and made me feel part of the club. Ever since that incident, Manchester City has been the only team for me.

But having said that, I must confess that the player who has made the greatest impression on me was George Best of Manchester United. To me he was better even than Pelé for he was so unorthodox, so skilful and he scored quite a few goals as well.

Another player I think highly of is Alan Ball, for when I first got into the City team at 17 I found myself playing against him, and he really gave me the run-around. He played a lot of one-two's and also first time passing, and it was so accurate thanks to his tremendous vision. And of course he was a very experienced player, even in those days.

I was born in St. Helens, on the 7th July, 1958—and my father played Rugby League—as a professional for Widnes.

But I always preferred football, and though I lived in St. Helens I was playing for the Warrington District Schools XI when Harry Goodwin, the former chief scout of Manchester City saw me and invited me to go to Maine Road. I signed a schoolboy form first, and then became an apprentice professional when I was 16.

As a youngster I played twice for the England Youth team against Wales, but because that was a qualifying match for the UEFA Youth competition and we were beaten over the two legs, that was all.

*Malcolm Allison, photo left, who put himself out to help Gary Owen when he was a schoolboy, and made a big impression on him.*

Then in season 1977–78 I was chosen for the England Under 21 team and in the European competition we reached the semi-finals before being beaten by Yugoslavia.

Last season I was still young enough for the Under 21 team and played again, and also played for the England 'B' team away to West Germany when we won 2–1. Then at the end of 1977–78 I also toured to Singapore, Australia and New Zealand with the 'B' squad under the Ipswich Town manager, Bobby Robson.

From my point of view the standard of play is improving in England for I am sure that England could have chosen three different under 21 teams that would have done equally well in Europe. That looks good for the future, but it was hard luck on some of the other very good young players who were left out.

Many good young players failed to get Under 21 caps simply because the team did so well and it was wisely decided to keep the team more or less the same.

My trip to the Far East with the 'B' team prevented me seeing most of the 1978 World Cup for we were

*Tony Woodcock scores the winning goal for England Under 21 v Italy. 'It was hard luck on many good young players because England did well, but could have chosen three equally strong teams', says Gary Owen.*

away at that time. But we returned just in time to see the final. I thought it was an excellent match, and I was very surprised by the Argentinians. Because of the experiences of European teams against Argentinian clubs, I think it was generally expected that they would be very rough and hard. But in fact they played with a lot of skill and had outstanding players in Osvaldo Ardiles and Mario Kempes.

This proved to me that if the Argentinian clubs had concentrated on playing football instead of rough-housing, they could have been a match for anyone in the world.

In 1974 I was at home and saw practically every match on television and was very impressed.

Clearly the English game is much different to that played abroad. For a start the English play quickly all the time. So the players in England have to hurry and scurry all the time and you have to use your skill to get over the furious pace of the game.

In continental European countries they tend to play at a more leisurely pace and mark man for man more tightly. So when they beat their man they have space before the next man can challenge and this gives them time to look around and think.

English defences are more compact, and if you beat one man here, another one is waiting for you, very close up. So in England there is no time to play the leisurely football as seen on the continent, and that is what makes the English First Division so competitive, and the strongest league in the world.

What I said earlier about the Argentines being very good when they decided to concentrate on playing football, also applies to the Italians. From what I saw of their national team it seems that their manager Enzo Bearzot is trying to cut out the physical stuff and also get them to concentrate on their skill rather than their well known defensive tactics. They too could do much better generally if they were to concentrate on playing football, for they have players with a lot of skill.

I played against Juventus for Manchester City and they were the hardest team to break down that I have ever met. They were also very physical too, which does not help their game.

Last season we also played against AC Milan in the UEFA Cup, and very surprisingly, they gave us a lot of space in the first leg in Milan. Usually Italian teams don't do that.

At Maine Road we scored an early goal against AC Milan to go ahead on aggregate, so they were forced to come out and attack and because of that we were able to win quite comfortably. Gianni Rivera, the Milan captain is in his mid-thirties but clearly he is still a very good player. He was a bit subdued in the second leg, but it was obvious that he was the leader of the orchestra, and thanks to his vast experience, his brain makes up for the things that his legs cannot do any more.

I specially admired Rivera because my game is basically that of an attacking midfield player, concentrating on the left side. Personally, I would always prefer to try to play creatively and in any case, I think my strength is in going forward, and I am not a very good defender.

The player I admire most at Maine Road however is goalkeeper Joe Corrigan for the way he has come back after almost leaving the club. At one stage he was overweight and out of form, but with tremendous dedication he got his weight down and improved his game through sheer hard work. Now he is playing really well and having played for England it seems clear that he is England's number three choice. But he had to work hard for it.

Another player that I get on very well with is left winger Peter Barnes. Of course he is also a very good player, but being roughly the same age, we are very good friends and always room together when travelling. He has been one season ahead of me all the way, joining City one year earlier and getting a Youth cap the season before I did.

Denis Tueart was also a very good winger, but of course he went off to the United States to play for the New York Cosmos. I think he was very wise, for he chose to put his wife and family before football, in order to secure his financial future.

*Joe Corrigan (photo right) is the City player most admired by Gary Owen because he has worked extremely hard for his success. Facing page shows Peter Barnes on the ball, who shares a room with Gary Owen when they are travelling with Manchester City.*

He realised that around 27 or 28 he had only limited chances of becoming an England regular, and receiving such a good financial offer he weighed it all up. Clearly he considered the British Tax structure which takes a large slice of a footballer's earnings, and his playing career is short enough anyway. So I am sure he made the right decision for him, because once you are past playing and step out of the game, you are forgotten.

But as far as I am concerned there is no chance of me going to the U.S.A. I still have to prove myself in English football, and I want that more than anything else. To prove myself a good player with Manchester City, help them to achieve all the honours going, and also, hopefully, to earn full caps for England.

Although I am still only 21 I am a considerably travelled young man, thanks to football. One of the places that I have found most exciting was Tokyo, because everything is so different there. The Ginza, Tokyo's famous shopping centre is a sight on its own.

Holland has also impressed me as a country with no rough and tumble that you find in most cities. Haarlem is a beautiful place, so clean and quiet with nice houses. We have visited Haarlem for pre-season matches twice in the last two years, and I really like it.

But of course, all the travel, and exotic places like Tokyo would be quite out of my reach if I were for example, working in a factory, so I owe all my travel opportunities to football.

Last season was almost a disaster for us however after we were expected to do well in all the competitions. Very largely, this was due to the fact that we got off to a poor start and were plagued by injuries. I was out myself for some weeks with an injured ankle, and very few of the players escaped injury, so we were unable to field a settled team.

Hopefully we shall come out of our lean spell, and as far as I am concerned all I want is to be a part of a successful Manchester City side, and if I am fortunate, to play for England.

*Dave Watson (right) is almost a veteran now in the City team but still an automatic choice for England.*

# Villa Need A Season Free From Injuries

*writes*

**GORDON COWANS**

PLAYING for a club with great traditions like Aston Villa can be both an uplifting experience, and also a bit frustrating. Uplifting because it is a great feeling to play before a big crowd of enthusiastic supporters, but frustrating when things don't go quite right.

It's nice to run out in front of a big crowd that are supporting you, though to be honest, once the game has started I find that concentrating on the game you tend to forget everything around you. You are too wrapped up in what is going on on the pitch to notice the fans, as long as they are for you.

There are times of course when the fans can get a bit impatient and you are aware of them then. I find this specially true as we walk off at half time, if we have been playing well and are on top but the score is still 0–0, because the supporters of course are expecting you to win, and tend to moan a bit, quite understandably, if we aren't winning.

Villa now have good enough players, and a big enough squad to make their mark on the game, but unfortunately, last season we had so many injuries that our game suffered. By the time the FA Cup started in January, every one of the first team players except goalkeeper Jimmy Rimmer and Ken McNaught had been injured and out of the side for at least one spell.

Personally, I broke a bone in my foot in a match against Notts Forest and was out for six weeks.

I've been with Aston Villa since I was sixteen and I'm a Villa man through and through.

I was born in West Cornforth, County Durham—on the 27th of October, 1958—but my family moved to Mansfield when I was small. When I was 13, someone from Villa saw me play and I was invited for trials and I stayed with the club and became first an apprentice professional when I was 16, and signed full pro at 18. So I have never known any kind of life except that of being a footballer.

I suppose football is in my blood, for though he was only an amateur, my father played the game.

In my early days I had a taste of international football, playing for the England Youth team, and of course I would be delighted to be chosen to play for the full England team.

England sent a team to play in the Youth Tournament in Monaco when I was 17 and I played three times in that competition. I was also chosen that season to play in the final stages of the European Youth Tournament, staged that year in Belgium. But I couldn't go because I was needed for Villa's first team.

*Jimmy Rimmer (facing page) was one of the few Villa players not seriously injured last season, and, photo above, another favourite at villa Park, John Gidman.*

Later I was one of the substitutes for the England Under 21 team in a competitive game against Denmark, so I am hopeful about further opportunities. With Aston Villa I was fortunate enough to be able to help win the Football League Cup, when we beat Everton in 1977. I didn't play at Wembley when the two teams drew 0–0, but I replaced Alex Cropley (who was injured) for the re-play at Hillsborough that was drawn 1–1. Because Frank Carrodus was unfit, I also played in the game at Old Trafford, when we finally clinched our success by 3–2.

One of our best players is Alex Cropley and he has been unfortunate in breaking a leg twice. I really rate him and enjoy playing with him, for when he is fully fit he works in midfield, challenging for everything; tackles well and has very good vision.

It's not the best way to do it of course, but I benefited from the misfortune that befell Alex. I was in and out of the side until he broke his leg and then I became a regular.

Dennis Mortimer is a key player in the Villa set up, a great driving force in midfield, and very strong going forward. Dennis also talks very well and gets you going, and he helped me tremendously when I first played and was the baby of the side.

But we have suffered a lot overall by the injuries to Andy Gray. He is the type of centre forward who can get goals from nothing and fights for everything. Andy is great in the air and generally very dangerous anywhere near the penalty area.

Having seen him score unexpected goals so many times, I am sure he is an inspiration to everyone, just as he is to me. The most important thing about Andy is that when he is playing, no matter if you are losing, you can still believe in yourself and the team, and that we can win . . . . . because Andy is likely to snatch a goal or two at any moment, even against the run of the play

*'Dennis Mortimer (facing page) is a great driving force for Villa', says Gordon Cowans and photo above, Alex Cropley, a fine player who has twice broken a leg.*

Our manager, Ron Saunders also plays a vital part in the Villa set up. He is not one of those managers who works in the office and only sees the players on match days. He is there at the training ground every day, working with the players.

Mr. Saunders has been of help to me in developing my game. If, for example the midfield has not been doing too well, he sets up things for the midfield players to work at in training and coaches them himself. He has the same approach to all three sectors of the team and obviously, working with the players all the time he gets the side to play the kind of football he wants, and I am sure it will bring a very deserved reward for we cannot have another run of injuries again, as we did last season. All we need to be in a position to challenge the most successful clubs is a run free of injury.

Kenny Swain has been an excellent acquisition and settled into our scheme of things right away when he joined us from Chelsea. I am sure he will prove to be a fine buy.

Overall the future looks good for Villa—barring injuries.

My role in the team is essentially that of an all-rounder, working up and down the pitch, according to the run of play, between the two penalty areas. I have to pick up one of our opponents too whenever the opposition gets posession, and though I feel I do my job quite well and am improving, I have found so far that the man most difficult to cope with is Liam Brady of Arsenal.

We have already had several very keen, individual battles and I really rate him as a player and thoroughly enjoy the battle of wits and skill with him.

FC Barcelona were the best foreign side Villa have met in my time and Johan Cruyff showed just what a great player he was when they drew 2–2 with us at Villa Park. I really thought we might have lifted the UEFA Cup that season for after being held at home by Barcelona we were winning 1–0 away when we had John Gidman sent off. You just cannot compete at that level with only ten men against a side like Barcelona at home and unfortunately we were eliminated.

Cruyff of course played a big part in the success of Holland in the 1974 World Cup and I was really impressed by them. Together with Argentina in the 1978 competition I think they are the best two sides I have ever seen, playing my kind of football really well.

Of the two I think Holland in 1974 were slightly the better side, for Argentina had the advantage of playing at home in 1978 and were 'lifted' by the big crowds of their own supporters. But both teams were really outstanding at world level.

Cruyff was unbelievably skilful, but as I have already said, the best player in Britain at the moment, is I think, Liam Brady. He is so difficult to play against for he drifts about everywhere, dropping really deep in search of the ball at times, and is consequently very difficult to pick up. And with the ball at his feet and coming at you, you cannot anticipate which side he is going to try to pass you on. He really is a handfull.

Liverpool are the outstanding team in England during my time, so consistent every week over a period of years. It is this consistency that we are aiming for, at Villa Park, but it has proved to be impossible having to change the side every week through injuries.

Having been very impressed by Argentina I really look forward to our games with Tottenham these days. It's a good feeling, knowing you are going to do battle with two of Argentina's World Cup squad and little Osvaldo Ardiles is proving himself a tremendous player.

I am all in favour of such players being signed by English clubs for stars like Ardiles help to swell the crowds and that can only be a good thing. Overall, such players add new interest to the game generally, and that can only be good for football in England.

*Andy Gray (photo left) who is an inspiration to other Aston Villa players because he can score goals even against the run of play, and (facing page), Gray's striking partner Brian Little who, with Gray, missed much of last season through injury.*

INTERNATIONAL GALLERY: SWEDEN

# SWEDISH FOOTBALL IN THE FORTIES

# REACHED ITS PEAK AND FIFTIES

*writes*
***LARS BERGSTRÖM***

☆ ☆ ☆ ☆

SWEDEN'S Fotbollforbund joined FIFA in 1907, though they had a national championship based on a Cup, knockout system, as early as 1896 and won for the first four years (and 9 times in the first 12 years) by the Gothenburg club Örgryte IS. The championship switched to a league system for the season 1924–25 and was won by GAIS (Gothenburg), and they changed the season to make soccer a summer game from spring to autumn in 1931. Since then the shape of Sweden's game has remained unchanged.

*Sweden's 1978 World Cup squad.*

*Two of the Swedish stars of the fifties (above). Left is centre half Åke Johansson, and right, centre forward Agne Simonsson.*

At international level, Sweden did not compete in the first World Cup, but eliminated strongly fancied Argentina in the 1934 series, beating them 3–2 in a first round match at Bologna. Then in 1938, Sweden reached the semi-finals, only to crash 1–5 to Hungary, but in 1950 they did remarkably well to be the most successful European side in Brazil, taking third place after Uruguay and Brazil.

By that time the Swedish game had already distinguished itself in 1948 by winning the Olympic Games soccer title in London, and doing it in fine style.

They were so impressive that Italian clubs whisked their biggest stars away immediately. Three of Sweden's forwards, Gunnar Gren, Gunnar Nordahl and Nils Liedholm all made great individual reputations as professionals in Italy, and for a spell they formed the inside forward trio of AC Milan.

Walking away with the championship, that Gre-No-Li team, as it is known, is still rated by many Italian experts as the finest club side ever seen in Italy.

Gunnar Gren was nicknamed 'il Professore', while Liedholm was a fine all-rounder and Gunnar Nordahl was a prolific, goal scoring centre forward.

But it says much more for Nordahl that in 1953 when the Austrian *maestro* Karl Rappan, who managed Switzerland to mini-miracles, was asked to choose and manage a Rest of Europe team to meet England at Wembley, he preferred Nordahl to the legendary Alfredo Di Stefano and then used him, not to score goals but to withdraw and lure the English centre half out of position so that the two inside forwards could score four times.

That AC Milan side with the Swedish inside forward trio was so good that they sparked off the Italian style of play now known as *catenaccio*.

Quite erroneously, the credit for introducing this system has been given to Helenio Herrera, but in fact it was the coaches of the lesser teams in Italy during the Milano 'Swedish era', that gave one of them the idea of double-marking Nordahl, Gren and Liedholm in order to prevent them scoring 8, 9 or 10 goals. Thus *catenaccio* was born.

Later, in October, 1959, Sweden were to become only the second continental team to beat England at Wembley, which they did by 3–2, but before that they produced what was probably their best ever team for the 1958 World Cup.

With Sweden staging the 1958 series after failing to qualify in 1954 using only home-based players, the Swedes pulled a master stroke. They did not start amongst the favourites, but with their home-based amateur team unbeaten 'in Sweden' for four years, they re-inforced their side by persuading the top Italian clubs to release Swedish players in time for them to train and prepare for the World Cup.

It came too late for Gunnar Nordahl who was past his best, but Gren and Liedholm, who was captain, formed an intelligent and skilful midfield partnership while the attack was spearheaded by two fine wingers, also back from Italy, Kurt Hamrin on the right, and Lennart 'Nacka' Skoglund.

The only home based forward in the line was Agne Simonsson, the centre forward who helped Sweden win at Wembley 18 months later, and signed for Real Madrid.

Sweden accounted for Mexico and Hungary in the first round and drew 0–0 with a strong Welsh team, before beating Russia 2–0 in the quarter finals. Then in the semi-final they accounted for the World Cup holders West Germany by 3–1 in Gothenburg, and earned the right to meet Brazil at their own Rasunda Stadium, at Solna, Stockholm, in the final.

After only four minutes Nils Liedholm gave Sweden the lead, but this was to prove a wonderful final in which Brazil fielded their strongest ever side, and finally, after a feast of entertaining football, the World Cup went to South America by five goals to two.

This was virtually to be the swan song of Swedish football for they failed to qualify in 1962 and 1966, and in 1970, 1974 and 1978 when they did reach the final stages, it was clear that their strength was now in defence and that they lacked the guile and skill of players like Gren and Liedholm and a super finisher in the class of Nordahl.

Ralf Edstrom flowered briefly as a striking forward, and spent what were probably his best years in Holland, playing for PSV Eindhoven, but the biggest stars of this period were goalkeeper Ronnie Hellstrom, voted Sweden's 'Footballer of the Year' for 1978 and who plays in the West German Bundesliga for 1st FC Kaiserslautern, and the *libero* Bjorn Nordquist, who retired from the game in Sweden at the end of 1978 with a world record, 115 international caps.

*A Swedish international team of the 1960s. Fifth from the left is centre back Bjorn Nordquist who went on to a World record 115 caps.*

*Ralf Edstrom (number 10, above) shoots at goal for Sweden against Brazil.*

The only forward in the 1978 team that made any impact was Thomas Sjoberg, the centre forward of Malmo FF. But after the World Cup he accepted a small fortune to go off and play in Saudi Arabia, and just how much even Malmo missed him is evident from their performance in the 1978 championship.

Under an English manager Bob Houghton, unknown in Britain, Malmo have been the leading Swedish club in the last four years. Oster IF (Idrottsforening) took the 1978 championship to Vaxjö, but in the previous four campaigns Malmo took the title three times.

The only club to 'nick' the championship from Malmo were Halmstad BK, and they too had an English manager, Roy Hodgson, when they won the league in 1976.

When Bob Houghton first took over the Malmo squad, many fans were unhappy that he introduced an English-style game, based on long passes and high crosses, and with the ball in the air more than usual. At first the crowds dwindled, but when it was seen to be successful they came swarming back to cheer the club to the championship. Malmo now rival Gothenburg, the traditional Swedish hot-bed of soccer, for high attendances.

IFK Goteborg were a big disappointment in 1978, the Swedes playing their championship from April to November. IFK had five internationals, including Bjorn Nordquist and Ralf Edstrom back from Holland, but it was Malmo that set the pace in the first half of the season.

When the Swedes broke off for their traditional summer break—so that the players can have holidays in the sun—Malmo had won eight and drawn one in their first nine games.

But then Malmo hit a bad patch and found goals hard to come by, and when Sjoberg flew off to Saudi Arabia this did not help in that department.

Malmo's remaining 15 league games brought only three wins, seven draws and five defeats, but such is the low general standard of play in Sweden that they still hung on to second place to qualify for the 1979-80 UEFA Cup.

As the season neared its end Malmo did even better. Thanks to a very tightly knit defence, they won the Swedish FA Cup, though significantly, in the final against Kalmar, the score after ninety minutes was 0–0. In extra time, Malmo scored the only goal and will now play in the European Cupwinners Cup instead.

Just four days before the FA Cup Final, Malmo qualified, as 1977 champions, for the last eight in the 1978-79 European Cup. Their opponents in the second round were the Russian club Dynamo Kiev, but clearly they have passed their peak. In Russia, Dynamo failed to score, drawing 0–0, and it was almost inevitable that Malmo should win at home—which they did by 2–0.

On paper it would seem that Malmo are a good side and that all is well with the Swedish game generally, even if they failed in the 1978 World Cup to look as good as they had in 1974 when they gave the ultimate winners, West Germany, a very good game.

In reality, the boom days of Swedish soccer have gone. There are no present day players who are even good enough to stand in the shadow of Gren, Nordahl, Liedholm and many more of their generation.

*International striker Benny Wendt who plays in West Germany.*

# ERNST POHL AND WLODZIM
# LIFTED POLISH FOOTBALL
# GRADE

# ERZ LUBANSKI
# NTO THE TOP

*writes*

*ERIC BATTY*

**I.F.B. Editor**

★ ★ ★

THE Polish Football Association was formed in 1919 and they joined FIFA in 1923. However, they played their first international, away to Hungary in 1921, and did well to lose by only 0–1, to one of the countries that had been quick to take to football and had already produced some fine players.

In the early days, Krakow was the centre of the Polish game, but in later years, Warsaw; with Legia, the Army team, and Polonia and Gwardia, also became a soccer centre.

But overall it seems clear that as in many other countries, there is an affinity between football and coal, and the majority of the Poles best players have been developed by the small town clubs around Kattowice, where they now play most of their big internationals at nearby Chorzow.

*Poland's 1978 World Cup team.*

Cracovia (Krakow) formed in 1906, were the first champions of Poland when the national league started in 1921, but that initial success was followed by Pogon, Lvov, now part of the U.S.S.R., taking the title four times in a row. Then in 1927 and 1928, Wisla Krakow were champions and were joined at the top by yet another Krakow club, Garbarnia, who took the title in 1931.

Now came the first of the champions from the Silesian coalfield when Ruch Chorzow took the championship four times in a row between 1933 and 1936, and remained one of the foremost clubs from then on.

Strangely, Poland's best known club is probably Gornik Zabrze who did not find success in the league until as late as 1957, though they soon established an all-time record by winning the title in five consecutive seasons.

It was Gornik, playing in a small, grimy coal town between Kattowice and Chorzow, who spearheaded Poland's drive into the hierarchy of the European game. In 1961 they gave Tottenham Hotspur a fright, for although they were well beaten in London, the first leg was a triumph for Gornik who were leading 4–0 until the final minutes, when the English club scored twice to make the score respectable.

The Gornik star at this time was inside left Ernst Pohl who scored a great goal against Spurs in London. He earned 49 caps for Poland between 1955 and 1965, scoring 40 international goals, and was certainly one of Poland's best players of all time.

With experience, Gornik developed, and in 1970 they reached the final of the European Cupwinners Cup. On the way they eliminated Glasgow Rangers, winning both at home and away by 3–1, but in the final they lost 2–1 to a very fine Manchester City team in Vienna. To date, this has been the best performance of any Polish club in European competition.

*A Gornik Zabrze team group (below) from the early 1960s. Second from the left in the front row is Ernst Pohl, with Wlodzimierz Lubanski on the extreme right.*

In the international arena, Poland first took part in the World Cup in 1938, eliminating Yugoslavia in the qualifying round, but went out in the first round proper to an excellent Brazilian team by the sensational score of 6–5, after extra time.

In the 1950's, Ernst Pohl found another extremely good player to complement his style in Lucjan Brychczy, an elegant player and fine dribbler who earned 60 caps between 1954 and 1969, and they spearheaded the Polish team to many international victories.

But at this stage in the development of the Polish game, Pohl and Brychczy piloted them to some high scoring victories against countries like Norway and other second rank sides, but against the old established professional countries, the Poles generally failed to make a mark.

In Pohl's later years with Gornik, the Zabrze club produced Wlodzimierz Lubanski who they signed from nearby GKS Gliwice and was first capped in 1963, when he was only sixteen. I first saw him in the 1960's when I visited Dr. Geza Kalocsai, an old Hungarian friend who was then coach of Gornik. It was immediately clear that Lubanski was an exceptionally gifted player, very skilful, quick and intelligent—and he scored goals too. He was to become the inspiration of Poland's national team, scoring almost a goal a game until he finally disappeared from the international arena after the 1978 World Cup, when he was clearly past his best.

At his peak Lubanski was fantastic, one of the best players in Europe, and not surprisingly Poland began to make a mark on the game at top level.

In conversation, Dr. Kalocsai had told me that bearing in mind that every team attacked at home, and defended away in the European Cup, it was easier . . . . to score goals, and win, *away from home.* When playing away, particularly if they were defending a two or three goal lead, everyone concentrated on defence and keeping possession of the ball, and if it was a revolutionary concept, Gornik made it work, with Lubanski the key man.

It would be wrong to suggest that Gornik were a one man team, but Lubanski was clearly the key player. If he played well then Gornik invariably won, but if he were kept controlled by tight marking—or foul play—Gornik inevitably suffered.

The theory of Dr. Kalocsai stood the rather severe test against Dynamo Kiev in 1967, when, in the first round proper of the European Cup, Gornik went to Russia and won 2–1. Then, at home, the Poles sat back and made the Russians come to them, and drew 1–1 to qualify.

After Dynamo Kiev, Gornik found themselves in a similar situation against Manchester United and away in the first leg, they tried once more to win at Old Trafford with quick counter attacks. United won 2–0, but both goals came very late in the game and tragically, Lubanski had shot over the bar from several good positions after Gornik had broken out and strung together several first time passes to open up the path to Alex Stepney. Then in Poland, a terrible pitch, covered with ice and snow, ruled out real football for the second leg, and though Gornik won 1–0 on the day, their best attempt yet at the European Cup was over, and Manchester United went on to win the trophy.

Lubanski, clearly, made a vital contribution to Poland's national team and their first success came in the 1972 Olympic Games. In the final in Munich, Poland beat Hungary 2–1 with Lubanski and Kazimierz Deyna providing an unanswerable combination at the heart of the Polish attack.

Although this feat was accomplished against fierce opposition from Hungary, East Germany and the Soviet Union, who all fielded very strong teams, little attention was paid to it in the West and in England in particular, where Poland were very sadly underestimated when England and Poland were drawn together in the same qualifying group for the 1974 World Cup.

Poland were destined to do very well indeed in the final stages where they took third place, but in England they were regarded as rank outsiders.

They began badly too, by being beaten 0–2 away to Wales in a match that was over-tough by any standards, but atoned by beating England by the same score in Chorzow. Unfortunately, Lubanski was carried off in that match and played no further part in the competition, sustaining a knee injury that needed two operations before he was able to play again. But Lubanski was never to be the same force again after this injury.

Poland's team was very well organised by manager Kazimierz Gorski, but he had some very fine players at his disposal. One of the key men was left winger

Robert Gadocha, who played in much the same style as John Robertson was to play later for Nottingham Forest, working in midfield, but also bursting forward as an orthodox winger when in possession.

In defence, Jan Tomaszewski proved to be an inspired goalkeeper, and no other defender did more for Poland than the *libero* Jerzy Gorgon, while the key figure after the departure of Lubanski was Deyna.

In the last match in the qualifying group, Poland were away to England at Wembley where it is still extremely difficult for visitors to do well. Poland were widely criticised, sometimes by figures in the game who should have known better, but in fact they deserved to win..

I had been more fortunate than most in seeing Poland play away to Bulgaria shortly before their visit to Wembley, and I had seen their new discovery, right winger Grzegorz Lato in all his glory. Though he was overweight, slower, and over the top by 1978, Lato in 1973–74 was a terrifying figure.

In full cry he moved like an Olympic sprinter, and he roved ceaselessly from his nominal position on the right wing, looking for goals. Later he was to underline just how good he was, by being the top goalscorer in the 1974 World Cup.

But at Wembley, he should have scored twice in the 1–1 draw that was enough to see Poland through. The first chance was spoiled when, due to inexperience, he hesitated, thinking he was off-side with England players appealing, and then, when the whistle didn't come, he found that the loss of vital seconds had enabled England goalkeeper Peter Shilton to get too far out of goal, and the opportunity was lost.

In the same match Lato broke through in the centre, only to be felled by a rugby tackle that robbed him of his second golden chance, and after Jan Domarski, the centre forward who stood in for Lubanski, had scored the opening goal, Poland hung on until the closing minutes when a very doubtful decision gave England a penalty from which they equalised.

But the 1–1 score-line was enough to put Poland in the finals by one point and when they were staged a few months later, Lato had been joined by another exciting striker, Andrzej Szarmach, who emerged as a free scoring centre forward in Poland's 1973–74 season and appeared as a surprise choice in the World Cup.

Though neither Lato nor Szarmach had the class and vision of Lubanski, they were temporarily amongst the most effective strikers in the game, and with seven goals and five goals respectively, were the top scorers in 1974.

Taking third place with a 1–0 win in Munich, over Brazil, with a well taken goal by Lato, Poland might even have done better had their critical quarter-final stage game against West Germany been played on a good surface.

For hours before this match the rain poured down and flooded the playing area, and though the pitch was covered with pools of water that made it virtually unplayable, the tight schedule of the World Cup made the referee decide to go ahead. The conditions were more against Poland than West Germany because the Poles built their attacks largely with ground passes, and with all the puddles such passes would not run true. Repeatedly the ball stopped dead in puddles, and in the end West Germany won the match 1–0 and went on to take the World Cup.

In 1978, only the newcomer Zbigniew Boniek proved to be a real force in the attack, while Lato and Szarmach showed that they had failed to maintain their form, and had gone back instead of becoming even better than they had been as young unknowns in 1974.

Poland failed in 1978, after qualifying in a first round group along with West Germany, but they will no doubt come again. Certainly the days when they murdered the minnows but crashed to the giants are over. Polish football is now firmly established in the forefront of the European game, and it was during the period 1971–1974 that they grew to maturity, when 'Wlodek' Lubanski was at his best.

What a tragedy that injury prevented him from becoming a household name. At an age when most players reach their peak, Lubanski spent two years out of action. He is revered in Poland, but the rest of the world did not see enough of him, for him to make a real impact, but without doubt it was he who played the critical role in putting Polish football firmly on the map.

*'Wlodek' Lubanski (dark shirt, facing page) in action against Bulgaria.*

# Brazilian forward play see have Lost its Craft and

# ns to
# Skill

*writes*

***ROBERTO da SILVA***

☆ ☆ ☆

THERE are depressing signs now that although the Brazilian game at home is still flourishing with occasional attendances of over 140,000 at the Maracana Stadium in Rio de Janeiro for league matches, and a nation-wide Cup competition also attracting enormous interest, it seems that in the international field, the Brazilian game has passed its peak.

In 1974, Brazil reached the World Cup semi-final and finished with fourth place, but that was very largely a defensive side, and what few stars there were, were in defence. Players like Luis Pereira and Francisco Marinho stood out, and they were both transferred to Spanish clubs. But they were both defenders. In addition, left back Marco Antonio, who looked like a class player on the 1973 European tour could not get in the side.

*A Brazilian line-up in a 1978 World Cup qualifying match.*

But in attack, particularly by comparison with former years, Brazil produced nothing new in the way of ideas, and precious little in terms of skill.

This trend was continued in the 1978 World Cup when team manager Claudio Coutinho claimed that 'as the only unbeaten side in the series, Brazil were as good as world champions.'

In fact the Brazilian attack failed miserably in 1978, and they were so short of attacking skill that in one match Coutinho fielded a right back on the right wing. And only when centre forward Reinaldo was brought into the side did the front three have any finishing power.

Yet Reinaldo is only a goalscorer, unlike even the most recent all-round centre forward, Tostao, who starred in the successful 1970 team. And overall, the most skilful attacking player was the midfielder Dirceu who was brought into the side only during the series in Argentina, and he was promptly transferred to a Mexican club after the World Cup.

For less than twenty years Brazil produced some of the world's best attacking players, but both before 1950 and after 1970, they had only the occasional star of real world stature.

Indeed, although the Brazilians took to futbol like ducks take to water, way back in the 1890's, they were overshadowed at international level by their neighbours to the south, Argentina and Uruguay.

Most of the clashes, prior to 1950, between Argentina and Brazil ended up in Argentina's favour, and Brazil did nothing to match the success of Uruguay in the 1928 Olympic Games and the 1930 World Cup. Argentina and Uruguay contested that 1930 final in Montevideo, Uruguay winning by 4–2, but Brazil failed to get past the first round, beaten 2–1 by Yugoslavia.

In the 1934 series Brazil were beaten by Spain, 3–1, again in the first round, and it was not until they were inspired by inside forward Leonidas in 1938 that they made any impact. Then they even struggled to beat Poland 6–5 after extra time, but did very well, again after extra time (1–1), when they eliminated the 1934 finalists, Czechoslovakia, by 2–1 in a replay.

Clearly improving as the competition developed, Brazil were eliminated by the eventual winners, Italy, but finally took third place with a 4–2 win over Sweden. Brazil had finally made a mark.

It will no doubt come as a surprise to many young readers, brought up on the legendary feats of Brazilian forwards like Pelé, to realise that although Brazil are still the only team ever to have won the World Cup three times, they did not achieve the honour of taking the crown for the first time until as late as 1958.

According to all logic, and the majority of critics of the period all agreed that Brazil had an outstanding team, and a fantastic inside forward trio; they should have won the World Cup in 1950 when the series was staged in Brazil.

After scoring 21 goals in the first five games, Brazil eventually failed in one of the biggest form upsets of all time. The inside forward trio, Zizinho, Ademir and Jair spearheaded Brazil's success and are still rated by the older critics to be the best trio of all time. But after reaching the final pool and then beating Sweden by 7–1 and Spain 6–1, they failed in the third and last, semi-final group game against Uruguay.

The Uruguayan side included several brilliant players like Andrade and Schiaffino, and the Uruguayans were still at that time a jinx team to Brazil. But the Uruguayans had only been able to beat Sweden by 3–2 and been in trouble against Spain with whom they drew 2–2. Now they had to beat Brazil, for a draw would have been enough to make Brazil the champions, and after being a goal down, that is just what Uruguay did, by two goals to one, and the entire population of Brazil was shattered.

The Brazilian fans had to wait eight more years before they were to win the World Cup in Sweden, and though they triumphed and were acclaimed in the end, and beat France 5–2 in the semi-finals and Sweden by the same score in the final, they got off to a very disappointing start.

Vicente Feola was the man in charge of the team, known as 'El Gordo' . . . the fat one. He developed the 4–2–4 system for Brazil, which, if it had been seen before, was never played so rigidly and so obviously until then.

The defence was settled and played well throughout, though the brilliant right back Djalma Santos, a

*The boy Pelé, watching a training game in 1958 with Vicente Feola behind him.*

survivor from 1954, was omitted until the final. Bellini, the captain at centre back was brilliant, while alongside him in the middle was the very reliable Orlando.

The first match proved to be a disaster for though they played 4–2–4, Feola's first choice attack failed miserably and could only draw 0–0 against England in Gothenburg.

Feola made changes, bringing in Zagalo on the left wing and Vava at centre forward. He also gambled on right winger Garrincha who had undergone an operation for appendicitis only six weeks earlier, and he produced the 17 years old Pelé, who had in fact been taken along, only to get the atmosphere in readiness for 1962.

Overall, the only forward to retain his place from the team that failed against England was inside right Didi.

Their first game together was against Russia which they won 2–0, and with Feola satisfied, the team settled down. The players became more and more accustomed to each other as the games went by, and the 'new' Brazil became a super-side of legendary fame.

Now Brazil were on top they stayed there, retaining the trophy four years later in Chile, with the same tactical formation and much the same team. Only Pelé was absent, injured in an early game, and inside left Amarildo came in for him, to get goals and become a star overnight.

The experts expected Brazil to win again in 1966, and if it has been said that they fielded a blend of players who were too old, veterans of 1958, and untried youngsters, they were not helped by the early injury to Pelé once more. But they were also still playing 4–2–4 while the rest of the world had advanced to 4–3–3. Thus Brazil's midfield duo were outplayed by other teams like Portugal and Hungary who played with three players in the middle of the park, and Brazil went home in disgrace once more.

For Mexico in 1970, the Brazilians qualified easily enough, but until former left winger Jorge Mario

*The brilliant Djalma Santos (left), and (facing page) Leao, perhaps the best goalkeeper Brazil has produced.*

Zagalo took over, just weeks before the big kick off, they were still playing 4–2–4.

Zagalo changed the tactics and re-shaped the side, and the result was another triumph for the genius of Brazil's attacking football.

Jairzinho on the right wing, blooded four years earlier, played like a black arrow and scored goals. Rivelino was given Zagalo's old role, dropping back from the left wing to work in midfield, and become an established star, going forward to produce his cannonball left foot shots, and in the centre of the attack they had Tostao and the veteran Pelé.

The defence caused flutters of worry from time to time, but Brazil won their first round group with victories over Czechoslovakia, Rumania and even won a difficult tie 1–0 against an England side that had a very strong defence and a brilliant goalkeeper in Gordon Banks.

In the quarter-finals the effervescent attacking skills of Peru were swept aside by four goals to two, and Uruguay were crushed 3–1 in the semi-finals.

The final in Mexico City was an intriguing affair with Brazil the acknowledged masters of attacking football, against the super-defensive Italy, and the 104,000 Azteca stadium saw a superb game. The first half ended all square at 1–1, but in the second half three more goals from a supremely skilful Brazilian attack took the Italians apart and demolished them.

Winners by 4–1, Brazil won the old World Cup outright.

But in the light of subsequent events, it now appears that the brilliant team of 1970 that produced a brand of attacking football that no one expected in an age when defences were on top in Europe, looks now to have been Brazil's swan song.

Jairzinho, Gerson, Tostao, Pelé, Rivelino!

That was the Brazilian attack, supplemented in midfield by the young Clodoaldo, and the equal of which has not been seen since anywhere. If it does transpire that the source of Brazil's brilliant attacking players has really dried up, then the world game will be the poorer, but they went out in style in 1970. playing the game the way it should be played.

# THE YEAR'S INTERNATIONAL FOOTBALL

BY the time this 21st edition of the International Football Book is on sale in the shops, the 1978 World Cup will be more than a twelve-month behind us. Some recollections of those long summer evenings of switching from BBC to ITV television channels to see some matches 'live' and the 'highlights' of others will be getting a bit hazy. No one can complain about the *extent* of the World Cup coverage in Britain on television but the *quality* was often disappointing. In Britain we have come to expect a very high standard, both of the camera work itself and of the producers understanding of the game.

Apart from the Argentinian TV's habit of repeatedly, whilst play was in progress, lingering over close-ups of various team managers or offering views of the crowd, the *flow* of the play often seemed to escape the cameras. I know that the best of all televised football can never expect to show the game as a whole. It must concentrate on the ball whereas spectators at the match can see both the ball and a wide area of the pitch around it, and therefore the movement of players not in the immediate vicinity of the ball. (Against that, as I expect all readers have experienced themselves when seeing the televised highlights of a match they had attended, the cameras do reveal incidents that were missed, or mis-seen, by spectators. The 'oohs' from the far end of the ground at what seemed to the spectators there to be only a narrow failure by a striker to reach a crossed ball near the goal, are seen on television to have been based more on hope than reality since the ball in fact was a couple of yards in front of the striker.)

There was some feeling of inevitability about the result when watching the Final itself between Argentina and the Netherlands. It is true that had Rensenbrink's shot that hit the upright in the closing minutes been just a couple of inches nearer the goal, the Dutch would have gone into a 2–1 lead and, with time so short, probably have held on. Instead, as I am sure you recall, first Kempes and then, with the Dutch players wholly committed to attack, Bertoni, gave the host country the world championship for the third time in the last four competitions. Once again too the Cup was won by a country from the continent in which the final tournament was staged. Only Brazil splendidly in 1958 have confounded the World Cup jinx.

Overall it was a disappointing final tournament and not helped by refereeing that fell some way below the level shown in the 1974 tournament in West Germany, and particularly in the later and most vital matches. Not for the first time, and not I expect for the last time, in World Cup final tournament, we saw teams that played attractively in the early matches fading whilst those who seemed to be struggling in early matches, improved as the tournament progressed. The expulsions in the last couple of minutes of the two Hungarian players, Nyilasi and Torocsik, came too late in the match for anyone to argue that the expulsions affected the result of Argentina's opening match 2–1 win over the Hungarians. (The loss of two players of whom they had expected much did, of course, weaken the Hungarians in their second match against Italy.) But throughout the match, and particularly after they had opened the scoring, the Hungarians, more than the Argentinians, had been confused and frustrated by the decisions of the Portuguese referee, da Silva Garrido, who himself seemed too conscious of the frenzied, partisan atmosphere in the stadium.

Scoring first in a match had not helped Hungary to a victory. Nor did it France in the same group (or Scotland against Peru for that matter!)—remember Lacombe's splendid first goal in the tournament (after West Germany and Poland had played a goalless match on the opening day)? But Italy scored twice to beat France and then France lost again by a similar odd-goal-in-three to Argentina. The French, as against Italy, had looked every bit as attractive as the Argentinians but all they had to show for their long overdue re-appearance in the final stages of a World Cup Competition was their third match win over Hungary.

The Argentinians for their part, with four points from their first two matches, were not unduly dismayed at losing one-nil to Italy—like the West Germans in 1974 they lost the match that did not matter! By the end of the first round matches however the prospect looked fairly bright for several European countries. Sadly France, with their richness of wingers at a time when most countries seem short of them, were out; as were the so disappointing Hungarians, Spain and Sweden, who had both drawn with Brazil but lost to Austria, then seen their own chances of advancing disappear when Brazil beat Austria; and, of course, Scotland. But Italy were looking sharp and the first three in the 1974 tournament, West Germany, Netherlands and Poland had all qualified for the Second Round, together with the surprising Austrians who fielded a strong defence and had in Krankl a valuable attacker.

There is always more to the final stages of the World Cup competition than playing matches. Who plays whom and when is a part of the game—and one can argue for hours the 'ifs' and the 'ands'. If, for example Argentina and not Italy had won the final match in their First Round group, then in the Second Round, Argentina would have had to play against West Germany, Austria and the Netherlands to reach the final, instead of, as happened, against Brazil, Peru and Poland.

At least the way the Second Round groupings worked out (and these are determined before the tournament starts, not by any draw—fixed or otherwise—when the actual qualifying countries are known) it prevented a repeat of the 1974 final since West Germany and the Netherlands were in the same group, and, unless Poland overcame the odds against them, it was virtually certain that the final would be a straight clash between a South American and a European country. Predictably the former were the Argentine, although only by goal-difference compared with Brazil, and the latter, the Netherlands.

I suppose all Europe were 'rooting' for the Dutch but for the second time they had to be content with second place. Now they must look to the 1980 European Football Championship. The Netherlands finished, you may remember, in third place in that remarkable 1976 European Championship when both semi-finals in Yugoslavia, the match for third and fourth places between the two beaten semi-finalists, and the Final itself all went to extra time. Even extra time was not enough to decide the winners—a penalty contest was necessary before Czechoslovakia beat West Germany, the holders. Nothing in the 1978 World Cup matched the skill, the excitement and the attacking emphasis of the 1976 European Championship

It remains to be seen whether the system that now applies will have the same salutary effect. Simply, in the past, the winners of eight qualifying groups (each contested on a home and away and a league basis) entered the knock-out (home and away legs) quarter-finals and the four winners of the quarter-finals took part in the final stages—semi-finals, 3rd/4th places, and Final held in the country of one of the four countries involved. Under the new system a host country is selected and that country automatically qualifies for a place in the final tournament which will be contested by eight countries (seven to qualify from groups) along the lines of the World Cup finals from the Second Round onwards. The main contenders to be the host country for the 1980 championship were Italy and England. On paper, even allowing that they had not entered for the first competition finalised in 1960, England had a strong case since Italy had already staged the final four matches in 1968, but there was an outstanding argument against England being invited to be the host country for the 1980 European Championship. Since the very successfully organized 1966 World Cup finals in England, the foul-mouthed hooligans that, at home and abroad, have presented an unacceptable face of British football have dissuaded UEFA from wanting to stage their championship in England. Indeed one wonders whether the F.A. could have been very keen on presenting England's case when at the back of their own minds they must have been nervous about the reaction of foreign football lovers to what they might experience attending matches here.

Italy, as the host exempted from qualifying, must

start as favourites to win the 1980 championship but for the rest of Europe the battle, already joined, is to qualify. Once again the 'seeding' system has failed to produce anything like evenly balanced groups and, far more than would a straightforward draw, has thrown up a number of repetitions. Once again, as for the 1976 championship, Poland and the Netherlands (both strong contenders in the 1974 and 1978 World Championships) are in the same qualifying group, whilst Spain, Rumania and Yugoslavia (joined this time by Cyprus) repeat their qualifying group for the 1978 World Cup.

Spain, who came from behind to qualify for the World Cup at the expense of Rumania when the final two matches saw Rumania beaten 4–6 at home by Yugoslavia and Spain winning one-nil in Belgrade, have, as I write, made a good start with a maximum six points from three matches. And one of those victories was away from home—against Yugoslavia. It can never be over-stated that qualification in these groups depends to a very large extent upon the points gained away (or, of course, as England know so well, qualification is lost by points lost at home).

There is another factor to be considered—goal-difference. The factor that took Italy and not England to Argentina. Wales were well aware of this when they hammered seven goals into Malta's net without reply but then came down to earth with a bump when they could only beat Turkey one-nil. That remark may not been quite fair to the Turks because although their 1978 paper record was poor—five matches played, one drawn and four lost, they had only been beaten by a single goal by Italy in Florence in September. As I write those two home Welsh matches are the only ones played in their Group Seven—the giant that had still to play was West Germany!

In other groups, the Netherlands have got off to a good start with three wins, including an away win against Switzerland; France won away in Luxembourg but had previously dropped a home point against Sweden, and the Swedes in their turn were beaten at home by Czechoslovakia. Czechoslovakia, the holders, in the course of a year of topsy-turvy form ended strongly by trouncing Italy 3–0 and only losing, perhaps against the run of the play, one-nil at Wembley against England.

Group Six promises to be decided by goal-difference—the Greeks seem to expect so at any rate. They lost their first match by three goals to nil in Helsinki, and lost the away match to the Soviet Union 0–2 but in their two home matches played to date beat Finland 8–1 and Hungary 4–1. Hungary, also beaten by Finland in Helsinki, beat the Soviet Union 2–0 in Budapest. The Soviet Union will be hoping to beat Finland by the same score as they did in a friendly in April 1978. Then the score was Soviet Union 10 Finland 2. Oleg Blochin scored four goals that day. He was not the only player during the international football year to score four in a match—Mavros did it for Greece against Finland, and Chester's Ian Edwards for Wales against Malta, but Blochin was the clear top goal-scorer in international matches for European countries. His tally was seven.

Scotland's chance of qualifying for the last eight has not been helped by the early matches—beaten in Portugal and in Austria and only odd goal (3–2) winners at home against Norway. Austria, encouraged by their historic win over West Germany during the World Cup in Argentina, seemed to be comfortably in the driving seat with their home win against Scotland and an away win against Norway—until they entertained Portugal. Portugal had started by dropping a home point against Belgium, who had themselves been held to a draw at home against Norway. Then Portugal went to Vienna and beat Austria and followed that with their home win against Scotland.

And what of England? Away to Denmark and the Republic of Ireland they have gathered three out of four points. Northern Ireland have the same catch for their two away matches against the Republic of Ireland and Bulgaria. It was a good win for the Irish in Sofia but it has to be admitted that, at the moment, Bulgarian football was at a low ebb. Their 1978 record was 12 matches played, none of them won, five drawn and seven lost. It is true that only two of the twelve matches were played at home but there was a significant absence of any semblance of a settled side. No fewer than 36 players appeared in those twelve matches. By the summer of 1979, when England visit Sofia, the Bulgarians may have stumbled upon a more successfully blended eleven but, even so, England should have picked up one, probably two, more points and, providing none are foolishly squandered at Wembley, should qualify.

Certainly, it is worth noting, their success rate (77·78%) was the best of the European nations in respect of matches played in 1978.

Mention of Bulgaria's chop-and-change 1978 line-ups reminded me of Yugoslavia's record over the past three years—in 1976, 33 players appeared in Yugoslavia's nine international matches; in 1977, 45 appeared in 12 matches and in 1978, 33 players in only five matches! Even Don Revie's selections for England could not match that!

I have not included Yugoslavia amongst the line-ups featured in the space available. Bulgaria are there and other countries, as Norway and Portugal for examples, that are in European groups with British countries.

As usual, the figures (1, 2, and even 3) after a position indicates a substitution but readers will appreciate that often there were positional changes involved—Nehoda, for example, is shown as the RH substitute for Jarusek for Czechoslovakia against East Germany. In fact Gajdusek moved from his one-time favourite left-wing place to midfield and Nehoda took over on the left wing. Unless otherwise stated the line-ups are in 4–3–3 formation—the exceptions are indicated by asterisks when it was known, or became apparent, that a different formation was being fielded. Football being a fluid and not a static game these formations need not be taken too literally but they can indicate whether a team set out to defend or to attack!

GORDON JEFFERY

# NORWAY

| | Date | Home | | Away | | Venue |
|---|---|---|---|---|---|---|
| A | 29. 3. 78 | Spain (Quini, Villar, Dani) | 3 | Norway | 0 | Gijon |
| B | 21. 5. 78 | Norway | 0 | Rep. of Ireland | 0 | Oslo |
| C | 31. 5. 78 | Norway (Thoresen) | 1 | Denmark (Arnesen, Larsen) | 2 | Oslo |
| D | 9. 8. 78 | Finland (Ismail) | 1 | Norway (Johansen) | 1 | Helsinki |
| E | 30. 8. 78 | Norway | 0 | Austria (Pezzey, Krankl) | 2 | Oslo (EFC) |
| F | 20. 9. 78 | Belgium (Cools) | 1 | Norway (Larsen) | 1 | Lokeren (EFC) |
| G | 25. 10. 78 | Scotland (Dalglish 2, Gemmill) | 3 | Norway (E. Aas, Okland) | 2 | Glasgow (EFC) |

| | A | B | C | D | **E | F | G |
|---|---|---|---|---|---|---|---|
| T. R. Jacobsen | G | G | — | G | G | G | G |
| Nygard | — | — | G | — | — | — | — |
| Karlsen | RB | RB | RB[1] | RB[1] | RB[1] | — | — |
| T. Jacobsen | — | RH[2] | RB[2] | — | — | — | LH[1] |
| Berntsen | — | — | — | RB[2] | RB[2] | CH | — |
| Kordahl | RH[2] | RCB[1] | — | LCB | — | RB | RB |
| Grondalen | RCB | — | RCB | — | LCB | LCB | LCB |
| Birkelund | — | RCB[2] | LCB | RCB | RCB | — | RCB |
| E. Aas | LCB | LCB | RH | RH | LH | RCB | CH |
| Pedersen | LB | LB | LB | LB | LB | LB | LB |
| Andersen | RH[1] | RH[1] | — | — | — | RH | — |
| Johansen | CH | LH | CH | CH | RCH | LH | RH |
| Thunberg | RF | CH | LH | LH | LCH | LF[2] | — |
| Ottesen | LH[1] | — | — | — | — | — | — |
| Hoyland | LH[2] | RF[2] | — | — | — | — | — |
| Hansen | — | — | — | — | — | — | LH[2] |
| Okland | — | RF[1] | CF[1] | LF | RF[2] | — | CF |
| Mathisen | — | — | RF | RF | RH | LF[1] | LF |
| Iversen | CF[1] | CF | CF[2] | CF[1] | RF[1] | — | — |
| Thoresen | — | LF[1] | LF | — | LF | RF | RF |
| S. Aas | CF[2] | — | — | CF[2] | — | — | — |
| Larsen | LF | — | — | — | — | CF[1] | — |
| P. Jacobsen | — | LF[2] | — | — | — | CF[2] | — |

**4-4-2

# AUSTRIA

| | Date | Home | | Away | | Venue |
|---|---|---|---|---|---|---|
| A | 15. 2. 78 | Greece (Galakous) | 1 | Austria (Krankl) | 1 | — Athens |
| B | 22. 3. 78 | Belgium (Geurts) | 1 | Austria | 0 | — Charleroi |
| C | 4. 4. 78 | Switzerland | 0 | Austria (Jara) | 1 | — Basle |
| D | 20. 5. 78 | Austria | 0 | Netherlands (Haan) | 1 | — Vienna |
| E | 3. 6. 78 | Austria (Schachner, Krankl) | 2 | Spain (Dani) | 1 | — Buenos Aires (WC) |
| F | 7. 6. 78 | Austria (Krankl) | 1 | Sweden | 0 | — Buenos Aires (WC) |
| G | 11. 6. 78 | Austria | 0 | Brazil (Roberto) | 1 | — Mar del Plata (WC) |
| H | 14. 6. 78 | Austria (Obermayer) | 1 | Netherlands (Rep 2, W. van der Kerkhof, Brandts, Rensenbrink) | 5 | Cordoba (WC) |
| I | 18. 6. 78 | Austria | 0 | Italy (Rossi) | 1 | — Buenos Aires (WC) |
| J | 21. 6. 78 | Austria (Krankl 2, one o.g.) | 3 | West Germany (Rummenigge, Holzenbein) | 2 | — Cordoba (WC) |
| K | 30. 8. 78 | Norway | 0 | Austria (Pezzey, Krankl) | 2 | — Oslo (EFC) |
| L | 20. 9. 78 | Austria (Pezzey, Schachner, Kreuz) | 3 | Scotland (McQueen, A. Gray) | 2 | — Vienna (EFC) |
| M | 15. 11. 78 | Austria (Schachner) | 1 | Portugal (Nene, Alberto) | 2 | — Vienna (EFC) |

| | A | B | C | D | **E | **F | **G | **H | **I | **J | K | L | M |
|---|---|---|---|---|---|---|---|---|---|---|---|---|---|
| Baumgartner | G[1] | — | — | — | — | — | — | — | — | — | — | — | — |
| Koncilia | G[2] | G[1] | G | G | G | G | G | G | G | G | — | — | G |
| Fuchsbichler | — | G[2] | — | — | — | — | — | — | — | — | G | G | — |
| Sara | RB | RB[1] | RB | RB | RB | RB | RB | RB | RB | RB | RB | RB | RB |
| Obermayer | — | RCB | RCB | RCB | RCB | RCB | RCB | RCB | RCB | RCB | RCB | RCB | RCB |
| Pezzey | RCB | LCB | LCB | LCB | LCB | LCB | LCB | LCB | LCB | LCB | LBC | LBC | LCB |
| Persidis | LCB | — | — | — | — | — | — | — | — | — | — | — | — |
| Strasser | LB | — | — | — | — | — | — | — | LB | LB | LB | LB | LB |
| Breitenberger | — | LB | LB | LB | LB | LB | LB | LB | — | — | — | — | — |
| Prohaska | RH | RH | RH | RH | RH | RCH | RCH | RCH | RH | RCH | CH | CH[1] | RH |
| Happich | CH | LH | — | LH[1] | — | — | LH[2] | — | — | — | — | — | — |
| Hickersberger | — | CH | CH | — | RCH[1] | RH | RH[1] | RH | LH | RH | — | — | — |
| Hattenberger | — | — | — | CH[1] | — | — | — | — | — | — | — | — | CH |
| Weber | LH | RB[2] | — | CH[2] | RCH[2] | RF[2] | RH[2] | — | — | — | RH | RH | — |
| Jara | — | — | LH | RF | LH | LH | LCH | LCH | — | — | LH[1] | RF | LH |
| Baumeister | — | — | — | LH[2] | — | — | — | — | — | — | — | — | — |
| Kreiger | — | — | — | — | — | RF[1] | LH[1] | LH | LCH | LH | — | — | — |
| Hintermaier | — | — | — | — | — | — | — | — | — | — | LH[2] | — | — |
| Oberacher | RF | RF | — | — | — | — | — | — | — | RF[2] | — | CH[2] | — |
| Schachner | — | — | RF | — | RF[1] | — | — | — | RF[1] | RF[1] | RF | CF | RF |
| Pirkner | — | LF[2] | — | — | RF[2] | — | — | — | RF[2] | — | — | — | — |
| Kreuz | — | — | — | LF | LCH | LCH | RF | RF | RCH | LCH | CF | LH | CF |
| Krankl | CF | CF | CF | CF | LF | LF | LF | LF | LF | LF | LF | LF | LF |
| Riedl | LF | LF[1] | LF | — | — | — | — | — | — | — | — | — | — |

**4–4–2

# BULGARIA

| | Date | Home | | Away | | Venue |
|---|---|---|---|---|---|---|
| A | 22. 2. 78 | Scotland (Gemmill, Wallace) | 2 | Bulgaria (Mladenov) | 1 | Glasgow |
| B | 29. 3. 78 | Argentina (Gallego, Ortiz, Ardiles) | 3 | Bulgaria (Grancarov) | 1 | Buenos Aires |
| C | 1. 4. 78 | Peru (Ramirez) | 1 | Bulgaria (Manolov) | 1 | Lima |
| D | 4. 4. 78 | Mexico (Ortega, Mendizabal, Lugo) | 3 | Bulgaria | 0 | Guadalajara |
| E | 23. 4. 78 | Czechoslovakia | 0 | Bulgaria | 0 | Brno |
| F | 26. 4. 78 | Poland (Lato) | 1 | Bulgaria | 0 | Warsaw |
| G | 3. 5. 78 | Rumania (Iordanescu, Balaci) | 2 | Bulgaria | 0 | Bucharest |
| H | 31. 5. 78 | Bulgaria (Mladenov) | 1 | Rumania (Iordanescu) | 1 | Sofia |
| I | 30. 8. 78 | East Germany (Eigendorf 2) | 2 | Bulgaria (Panov, A. Stankov) | 2 | Erfurt |
| J | 20. 9. 78 | Italy (Cabrini) | 1 | Bulgaria | 0 | Turin |
| K | 11. 10. 78 | Denmark (B. Nielsen, Lerby) | 2 | Bulgaria (Panov 2) | 2 | Copenhagen (EFC) |
| L | 29. 11. 78 | Bulgaria | 0 | N. Ireland (Armstrong, Caskey) | 2 | Sofia (EFC) |

| | A | B | C | D | E | F | G | H | **I | **J | K | L |
|---|---|---|---|---|---|---|---|---|---|---|---|---|
| Stajkov | G | G | G | — | G | G | G | G | G | — | G | — |
| Zafirov | — | — | — | G | — | — | — | — | — | — | — | — |
| Goranov | — | — | — | — | — | — | — | — | — | G | — | G |
| Nikolov | RB | — | — | RB | — | — | RB | RB | RB | RB | RB | — |
| Grancarov | — | RB | RB | — | LCB | — | LCB | LCB | — | — | RCB | RB |
| Mincev | — | — | — | — | RB | RB | — | — | — | — | — | — |
| Encev | RCB | — | — | — | — | — | — | — | — | — | — | — |
| Marev | — | RCB | LCB | RCB | — | — | — | — | — | — | — | — |
| Iljev | LCB | LCB[1] | RCB | — | — | LCB | — | — | — | LCB | — | — |
| Dimitrov | — | — | — | — | RCB | RCB | RCB | — | — | — | — | LB |
| Tisanski | LH[2] | RH | RF | LH | RH | RH | CH | RCB | RH | — | — | — |
| P. Stankov | — | — | — | — | — | — | — | — | RCB | RCB | LCB | RCB |
| Bonev | LB | LB | LH | LCB | LB | LB | LB | LB | LB | LB | RH | — |
| Dzevizov | — | — | — | — | — | — | — | — | LCB | LH | — | RF[2] |
| Karakolev | — | — | — | — | — | — | — | — | — | — | — | LCB |
| Kaserov | RH | LH | LB | LB | — | — | RH[1] | — | — | RH | — | — |
| Ivanov | CH | — | — | — | — | — | RF | CH[1] | LCH | LCH[1] | LB | — |
| Manolov | — | RF | RH[1] | CH[2] | CF | CF[1] | CF[2] | — | — | — | — | — |
| Milkov | — | LF[2] | — | RH | — | — | RH[2] | LF[2] | — | — | — | — |
| Zdravkov | LF | — | — | — | — | — | LH | RH | — | RCH | — | — |
| Stretkov | — | — | — | — | — | — | — | — | — | — | — | RH |
| Denev | — | CH | — | — | — | — | — | — | — | — | — | — |
| Markov | — | LCB[2] | CH | RF | CH[1] | CH | — | — | RCH[2] | LCH[2] | — | — |
| Petrov | — | — | — | CH[1] | — | — | — | — | — | — | — | — |
| Slavkov | LH[1] | — | — | — | — | — | — | LH | RCH[1] | — | LH | LH |
| Gocev | — | — | — | — | — | — | — | — | — | LF[2] | LF | CH |
| Mincev | — | — | — | — | LH | LH | — | — | — | — | — | — |
| Panov | — | — | — | — | — | — | — | — | LH | RF | CF | LF |
| Zeljazkov | RF | CF | RH[2] | — | — | — | — | — | — | — | — | — |
| Kolev | — | — | — | — | RF[1] | — | — | — | — | — | — | — |
| A. Stankov | — | — | — | — | RF[2] | LF | CF[1] | — | RF | LF[1] | CH | CF[1] |
| Metodijev | — | — | CF | CF | CH[2] | RF | — | CH[2] | — | — | — | — |
| Kocev | — | — | — | — | LF[2] | — | — | RF | — | — | — | — |
| Mladenov | CF | — | — | — | — | — | — | CF | LF | — | RF | RF[1] |
| Cvetkov | — | LF[1] | LF | LF | LF[1] | CF[2] | LF | — | — | — | — | CF[2] |
| Spasov | — | — | — | — | — | — | — | LF[1] | — | — | — | — |

**4-4-2

# ENGLAND

| | Date | Home | Away | Venue |
|---|---|---|---|---|
| A | 22. 2. 78 | West Germany ............2 (Worm, Bonhof) | England ..................1 (Pearson) | — Munich |
| B | 19. 4. 78 | England ..................1 (Keegan) | Brazil ....................1 (Gil) | — Wembley |
| C | 13. 5. 78 | Wales ....................1 (Dwyer) | England ..................3 (Latchford, Currie, Barnes) | — Cardiff (BHC) |
| D | 16. 5. 78 | England ..................1 (Neal) | N. Ireland ...............0 | — Wembley (BHC) |
| E | 20. 5. 78 | Scotland ..................0 | England ..................1 (Coppell) | — Glasgow (BHC) |
| F | 24. 5. 78 | England ..................4 (Barnes, Neal, Francis, Currie) | Hungary ..................1 (Nagy) | — Wembley |
| G | 20. 9. 78 | Denmark ..................3 (Simonsen, Arnesen, Roentved) | England ..................4 (Keegan 2, Latchford, Neal) | — Copenhagen (EFC) |
| H | 25. 10. 78 | Rep. of Ireland ............1 (G. Daly) | England ..................1 (Latchford) | — Dublin (EFC) |
| I | 29. 11. 78 | England ..................1 (Coppell) | Czechoslovakia ............0 | — Wembley |

| | *A | *B | *C | D | *E | *F | *G | *H | **I |
|---|---|---|---|---|---|---|---|---|---|
| Clemence ........ | G | — | — | G | G | — | G | G | — |
| Corrigan ......... | — | G | — | — | — | — | — | — | — |
| Shilton .......... | — | — | G | — | — | G | — | — | G |
| Neal ............ | RB | — | — | RB | RB | RB | RB | RB | — |
| Mills ............ | LB | RB | RB | LB | LB | LB | LB | LB | — |
| Anderson ........ | — | — | — | — | — | — | — | — | RB |
| Cherry .......... | — | LB | LB[1] | — | — | — | — | — | LB |
| Watson .......... | RCB | RCB | RCB | RCB | RCB | RCB[1] | RCB | RCB[1] | LCB |
| Thompson ....... | — | — | — | — | — | — | — | RCB[2] | RCB |
| Hughes .......... | LCB | — | — | LCB | LCB[1] | LCB | LCB | LCB | — |
| B. Greenhoff...... | — | LCB | LCB | LH | LCB[2] | RCB[2] | — | — | — |
| Wilkins .......... | RH | — | RH | RH | RH | RH | RH | RH | RH |
| Currie ........... | — | RH | LB[2] | CH | LH | OR[2] | — | — | LCH |
| Brooking ......... | LH | — | LH | — | LCF[2] | LH | LH | LH | — |
| Keegan .......... | LCF[1] | LH | — | — | — | LCF | LCF | LCF | LH |
| Coppell .......... | OR | OR | OR | RF | OR | OR[1] | OR | OR | RCH |
| Pearson .......... | RCF | — | — | CF | — | — | — | — | — |
| Latchford ........ | — | RCF | LCF[1] | — | — | — | RCF | RCF | RF[2] |
| T. Francis........ | LCF[2] | LCF | RCF | — | RCF | RCF | — | — | — |
| Mariner ......... | — | — | LCF[2] | — | LCF[1] | — | — | — | — |
| Woodcock ....... | — | — | — | LF | — | — | — | OL[2] | RF[1] |
| Barnes........... | OL | OL | OL | — | OL | OL | OL | OL[1] | LF |

*4-2-4
**4-4-2

# WALES

| | Date | Home | Away | Venue |
|---|---|---|---|---|
| A | 18. 4. 78 | Iran ......................0 | Wales ....................1 (Dwyer) | — Tehran |
| B | 13. 5. 78 | Wales ....................1 (Dwyer) | England ..................3 (Latchford, Currie, Barnes) | — Cardiff (BHC) |
| C | 17. 5. 78 | Scotland ..................1 (Johnstone) | Wales ....................1 (Donachie o.g.) | — Glasgow (BHC) |
| D | 19. 5. 78 | Wales ....................1 (Deacy) | Northern Ireland ..........0 | — Wrexham (BHC) |
| E | 25. 10. 78 | Wales ....................7 (Edwards 4, O'Sullivan, Thomas, Flynn) | Malta ....................0 | — Wrexham (EFC) |
| F | 29. 11. 78 | Wales ....................1 (Deacy) | Turkey ...................0 | — Wrexham (EFC) |

| | A | B | C | D | *E | *F |
|---|---|---|---|---|---|---|
| Davies | G | G | G | G | G | G |
| Page | RB | RB | RB | — | RCB | — |
| Davis | RCB | LCB[2] | — | RCB | — | — |
| Phillips | — | RCB | RCB | — | LCB | RCB |
| D. Jones | LCB | LCB[1] | — | — | — | — |
| Roberts | — | — | LCB | LCB | — | — |
| J. Jones | LB | LB | LB | LB | LB | LB |
| Mahoney | RH[1] | RH[2] | LH | LH | — | — |
| Flynn | RH[2] | CH | CH | CH | RH | RH |
| Yorath | CH | RH[1] | RH | RH[1] | — | LCB |
| Stevenson | — | — | — | RB | RB | RB |

| | A | B | C | D | *E | *F |
|---|---|---|---|---|---|---|
| Harris | RF[1] | RF | RF | RF | OR | OR |
| M. Thomas | LH | LH | — | RH[2] | LH | LH |
| Cartwright | RF[2] | — | — | — | OL[1] | — |
| Dwyer | CF | LF | LF[1] | CF | — | RCF |
| Curtis | — | CF | CF | — | — | — |
| Edwards | — | — | — | — | RCF | — |
| R. James | — | — | — | — | LCF | — |
| Deacy | LF | — | LF[2] | LF | — | LCF |
| O' Sullivan | — | — | — | — | OL[2] | — |
| L. James | — | — | — | — | — | OL |

*4-2-4

# CZECHOSLOVAKIA

| | Date | Home | | Away | | Venue |
|---|---|---|---|---|---|---|
| A | 22. 3. 78 | Greece | 0 | Czechoslovakia (Kroupa) | 1 | Salonika |
| B | 15. 4. 78 | Hungary (Nyilasi, one o.g.) | 2 | Czechoslovakia (Kroupa) | 1 | Budapest |
| C | 23. 4. 78 | Czechoslovakia | 0 | Bulgaria | 0 | Brno |
| D | 17. 5. 78 | Brazil (Reinaldo, Zico) | 2 | Czechoslovakia | 0 | Rio |
| E | 21. 5. 78 | Sweden | 0 | Czechoslovakia | 0 | Stockholm |
| F | 6. 9. 78 | East Germany (Pommerenke, Eigendorf) | 2 | Czechoslovakia (Ondrus) | 1 | Leipzig |
| G | 4. 10. 78 | Sweden (Borg) | 1 | Czechoslovakia (Masny, Kroupa, Nehoda) | 3 | Stockholm (EFC) |
| H | 11. 10. 78 | Czechoslovakia (Stambachr 2, Masny) | 3 | West Germany (Abramczik, Bonhof 2, H. Muller) | 4 | Prague |
| I | 8. 11. 78 | Czechoslovakia (Jarusek, Panenka, Masny) | 3 | Italy | 0 | Bratislava |
| J | 29. 11. 78 | England (Coppell) | 1 | Czechoslovakia | 0 | Wembley |

| | A | B | C | D | **E | F | G | H | I | J |
|---|---|---|---|---|---|---|---|---|---|---|
| Hruska | G[1] | — | G | G | — | — | — | — | — | — |
| Netolicka | G[2] | G | — | — | G | — | — | — | — | — |
| Keketi | — | — | — | — | — | G | — | — | — | — |
| Michalik | — | — | — | — | — | — | G | G | G | G |
| Barmos | RB | RB | RB | RB | RB | RB | RB | RB | RB | RB |
| Ondrus | RCB | — | — | RCB | RCB | RCB | RCB | RCB | RCB | — |
| Dobias | — | RCB | RCB | — | — | — | — | — | — | — |
| Vojacek | — | — | — | — | — | — | LCB | LCB | LCB | RCB |
| Prokes | LCB | — | — | — | — | — | — | — | — | — |
| Fiala | — | LCB | LCB | LCB | LCB | LCB | — | — | LB[2] | — |
| Jurkemik | — | — | — | — | — | — | — | — | — | RCB |
| Gogh | LB | LB[1] | LB | LB | LB | LB | LB | LB | LB[1] | LB |
| Samek | — | LB[2] | — | — | — | — | — | — | — | — |
| Jarusek | RH[1] | LH | CH | CH | RCH | RH[1] | — | — | CH[1] | CH[1] |
| Kozak | RH[2] | CH[2] | RH | LH[1] | RH[1] | LH | CF[2] | RH[2] | RH | RH |
| Bilsky | CH | RH | LH[1] | RH[1] | LCH | CF[2] | — | — | — | — |
| Rott | — | — | — | RH[2] | — | — | — | CF[2] | — | — |
| Vizek | — | — | — | — | RH[2] | — | — | — | — | — |
| Pollak | — | — | — | — | — | CH | RH | RH[1] | — | — |
| Panenka | LH | CH[1] | LH[2] | — | — | — | — | LH[2] | CH[2] | CH[2] |
| Stambachr | — | — | — | — | — | | CH | CH | LH | LH |
| Gajdusek | RF[2] | — | — | LH[2] | LH | LF | LH | LH[1] | LF | LF |
| Masny | RF[1] | RF[2] | RF | RF | RF | RF | RF | RF | RF | RF |
| Janecka | — | RF[1] | LF[2] | — | — | — | — | — | — | — |
| Kroupa | CF | CF | CF | CF | LF[1] | — | CF[1] | CF[1] | — | — |
| Kloucek | — | — | — | — | — | CF[1] | — | — | — | — |
| Nehoda | LF | LF | LF[1] | LF | LF[2] | RH[2] | LF | LF | CF | CF |

**4-4-2

# FRANCE

A 8. 2. 78 Italy ......................2 France ....................2 — Naples
(Graziani 2) (Bathenay, Platini)

B 8. 3. 78 France ....................2 Portugal ..................o — Paris
(Baronchelli, Berdoll)

C 1. 4. 78 France ....................1 Brazil .....................o — Paris
(Platini)

D 11. 5. 78 France ....................2 Iran ......................1 — Toulouse
(Gemmrich, Six) (Rowshan)

E 19. 5. 78 France ....................2 Tunisia ....................o — Lille
(Platini, Dalger)

F 2. 6. 78 Italy ......................2 France ....................1 — Mar del Plata (WC)
(Rossi, Zaccarelli) (Lacombe)

G 6. 6. 78 Argentina..................2 France ....................1 — Buenos Aires (WC)
(Passarella, Luque) (Platini)

H 10. 6. 78 France ....................3 Hungary ..................1 — Mar del Plata (WC)
(Lopez, Berdoll, Rocheteau) (Zombori)

I 1. 9. 78 France ....................2 Sweden....................2 — Paris (EFC)
(Berdoll, Six) (Larsson, Nordgren)

J 7. 10. 78 Luxembourg...............1 France ....................3 — Luxembourg (EFC)
(Michaud) (Six, Tresor, Gemmrich)

K 8. 11. 78 France ....................1 Spain .....................o — Paris
(Specht)

| | A | B | C | D | E | F | G | H | I | J | K |
|---|---|---|---|---|---|---|---|---|---|---|---|
| Rey ........... | G | G | — | — | — | — | — | — | G | — | — |
| Bertrand-Demanes | — | — | G | G | G | G | G[1] | — | — | — | — |
| Baratelli ........ | — | — | — | — | — | — | G[2] | — | — | — | — |
| Dropsy ......... | — | — | — | — | — | — | — | G | — | G | G |
| Janvion ........ | RB | RB | — | RB | LB | RB | — | RB | — | — | LB |
| Battiston ....... | — | RCB[2] | RB[1] | — | RB | — | RB | — | RB | RB | RB |
| Bracci.......... | — | — | RB[2] | — | RCB[2] | — | — | LB | — | — | — |
| Rio............. | RCB[1] | LCB | LCB | RCB | RCB[1] | LCB | — | — | LCB | — | — |
| Lopez.......... | RCB[2] | RCB[1] | RCB | LCB[2] | LCB | — | LCB | LCB | RCB | LCB | RCB |
| Tresor ......... | LCB | — | — | LCB[1] | — | RCB | RCB | RCB | — | RCB | — |
| Specht ......... | — | — | — | — | — | — | — | — | — | — | LCB |
| Bossis .......... | LB | LB | LB | LB | — | LB | LB | — | LB | LB | — |
| Platini........... | RH | — | LH | — | LH[2] | CH | LH | LH[2] | — | — | — |
| Sahnoun ....... | — | RH | — | RH[1] | — | — | — | — | — | — | — |
| Michel ......... | LH[2] | CH | RH[1] | CH | — | RH | CH | — | CH | — | RH |
| Petit ........... | — | — | RH[2] | — | RH | — | — | RH | — | CH[2] | CH |
| Bathenay ....... | CH | — | — | RH[2] | CH | — | RH | CH | RH | — | — |
| Jouve .......... | — | — | — | — | — | — | — | — | LH[1] | RH | — |
| Guillou ........ | LH[1] | — | CH | — | LH[1] | LH | — | — | — | — | — |
| Larios.......... | — | — | — | — | — | — | — | — | — | CH[1] | — |
| Giresse ......... | — | LH | — | — | — | — | — | — | LH[2] | — | — |
| Keruzore ....... | — | — | — | LH | — | — | — | — | — | — | — |
| Papi ........... | — | — | — | — | — | — | — | LH[1] | — | — | — |
| Piasecki ........ | — | — | — | — | — | — | — | — | — | LH | LH |
| Dalger ......... | RF | — | — | — | RF | RF | — | — | — | — | — |
| Baronchelli ..... | — | RF | RF | — | — | — | — | — | — | — | — |
| Rocheteau ...... | — | — | — | RF | — | — | RF | RF[1] | — | RF[1] | RF[1] |
| Six ............ | — | LF | LF[2] | LF[2] | LF[1] | LF[1] | LF | RF[2] | LF | LF | LF |
| Gemmrich ...... | LF[2] | — | — | LF[1] | — | — | — | — | CF[1] | RF[2] | RF[2] |
| Soler............. | — | — | — | — | — | — | — | — | — | — | CF[2] |
| Lacombe ........ | CF | — | — | CF[1] | CF[2] | CF[1] | CF | — | — | CF | — |
| Berdoll ......... | — | CF[1] | CF | CF[2] | CF[1] | CF[2] | — | CF | CF[2] | — | — |
| Amisse ......... | — | CF[2] | LF[1] | — | — | — | — | — | — | — | — |
| Pleinmelding .... | — | — | — | — | — | — | — | — | — | — | CF[1] |
| Rouyer......... | LF[1] | — | — | — | LF[2] | LF[2] | — | LF | RF | — | — |

# WEST GERMANY

| | Date | Home | | Away | | Venue |
|---|---|---|---|---|---|---|
| A | 22. 2. 78 | West Germany (Worm, Bonhof) | 2 | England (Pearson) | 1 | Munich |
| B | 8. 3. 78 | West Germany (Russmann) | 1 | Soviet Union | 0 | Frankfurt |
| C | 5. 4. 78 | West Germany | 0 | Brazil (Nunes) | 1 | Hamburg |
| D | 19. 4. 78 | Sweden (L. Larsson 2, one o.g.) | 3 | West Germany (Bonhof) | 1 | Stockholm |
| E | 1. 6. 78 | West Germany | 0 | Poland | 0 | Buenos Aires (WC) |
| F | 6. 6. 78 | West Germany (D. Muller, H. Muller, Rummenigge 2, Flohe 2) | 6 | Mexico | 0 | Cordoba (WC) |
| G | 10. 6. 78 | West Germany | 0 | Tunisia | 0 | Cordoba (WC) |
| H | 14. 6. 78 | West Germany | 0 | Italy | 0 | Buenos Aires (WC) |
| I | 18. 6. 78 | West Germany (Abramczik, D Muller) | 2 | Netherlands (Haan, R. van der Kerkhof) | 2 | Cordoba (WC) |
| J | 21. 6. 78 | Austria (Krankl 2, one o.g.) | 3 | West Germany (Rummenigge, Holzenbein) | 2 | Cordoba (WC) |
| K | 11. 10.78 | Czechoslovakia (Stambachr 2, Masny) | 3 | West Germany (Abramczik, Bonhof 2, H. Muller) | 4 | Prague |
| L | 20. 12. 78 | West Germany (Rummenigge, Fischer, Bonhof) | 3 | Netherlands (La Ling) | 1 | Dusseldorf |

*(The match between West Germany and Hungary in Frankfurt on 15 November was abandoned after 60 minutes owing to fog. No goals had been scored.)*

| | A | B | C | D | **E | F | **G | **H | **I | J | K | L |
|---|---|---|---|---|---|---|---|---|---|---|---|---|
| Maier | G | G | G | G[1] | G | G | G | G | G | G | G | — |
| Burdenski | — | — | — | G[2] | — | — | — | — | — | — | — | G |
| Vogts | RB | RB | RB | RB | RB | RB | RB | RB | RB | RB | — | — |
| Schwarzenbeck | RCB | — | — | — | — | — | — | — | — | — | — | — |
| Kaltz | — | RCB | RCB | RCB | RCB | RCB | RCB | RCB | RCB | RCB | RB | RB |
| Forster | — | — | LB[2] | — | — | — | — | — | — | — | RCB | — |
| Russmann | LCB | LCB | LCB | LCB | LCB | LCB | LCB | LCB | LCB | LCB | — | — |
| Zewe | — | — | — | — | — | — | — | — | — | — | LCB | LCB |
| Zimmermann | LB | — | — | LB | LB | — | — | LCH[1] | — | — | — | CH[2] |
| Dietz | LH[2] | LB[1] | LB | RH[2] | — | LB | LB | LB | LB | LB | LB | LB |
| Bonhof | RH | RH | RH | RH[1] | RCH | RH | RH | RH | RH | RH | RH | RCB |
| Flohe | CH[1] | CH | CH | — | RH | CH | RCH | RCH[1] | — | — | — | — |
| Stielike | — | — | — | — | — | — | — | — | — | — | — | RH |
| Burgsmuller | CH[2] | — | — | — | — | — | — | — | — | — | — | — |
| Holzenbein | CF[1] | LH | — | CH | — | — | — | LH | LCH | LH | — | — |
| Beer | — | — | LH[1] | — | LCH | — | — | RCH[2] | RCH | CH[1] | — | — |
| H. Muller | — | — | RF[2] | LH[1] | LH | LH | LH | — | — | CH[2] | LF[1] | — |
| Neumann | LH[1] | — | — | — | — | — | — | — | — | — | — | — |
| Worm | CF[2] | — | LH[2] | LH[2] | — | — | — | — | — | — | LF[2] | — |
| Konopka | — | — | — | — | — | — | — | LCH[2] | — | — | — | — |
| Cullmann | — | — | — | — | — | — | — | — | — | — | CH | CH[1] |
| K. Allofs | — | — | — | — | — | — | — | — | — | — | LF[3] | LH |
| Abramczik | RF | RF | RF[1] | RF | RF | — | — | — | RF | RF | RF | RF[1] |
| Rummenigge | LF | LF | LF | LF | — | RF | LCH | RF | LH | LF | LH | LF |
| Fischer | — | CF | CF | CF | LF | CF | RF | LF | — | CF[2] | CF | CF |
| D. Muller | — | — | — | — | — | LF | LF | — | LF | CF[1] | — | — |
| Borchers | — | — | — | — | — | — | — | — | — | — | — | RF[2] |

**4-4-2

# GREECE

| |  | | | | |  |
|---|---|---|---|---|---|---|
| A | 11. 1. 78 | Cyprus | 0 | Greece (Mavros, Galakous) | 2 | — Nicosia |
| B | 15. 2. 78 | Greece (Galakous) | 1 | Austria (Krankl) | 1 | — Athens |
| C | 22. 3. 78 | Greece | 0 | Czechoslovakia (Kroupa) | 1 | — Salonika |
| D | 5. 4. 78 | Poland (Deyna 2, Lato, Zmuda, Boniek) | 5 | Greece (Karavitis, Mavros) | 2 | — Poznan |
| E | 25. 5. 78 | Finland (Ismail 2, Nieminen) | 3 | Greece | 0 | — Helsinki (EFC) |
| F | 20. 9. 78 | Soviet Union (Chesnokov, Bessonov) | 2 | Greece | 0 | Erevan (EFC) |
| G | 11. 10. 78 | Greece (Mavros 4, Delikaris 2, Galakous, Nikoloudis) | 8 | Finland (Heikanen) | 1 | — Athens (EFC) |
| H | 29. 10. 78 | Greece (Galakous 2, Mavros Ardizoglou) | 4 | Hungary (Varadi) | 1 | — Salonika (EFC) |
| I | 15. 11. 78 | Yugoslavia (Halihodzic 3, Savic) | 4 | Greece (Mavros) | 1 | — Skopje |
| J | 13. 12. 78 | Greece (Koudas Nikoloudis) | 2 | Rumania (Augustin) | 1 | — Athens |

| | A | B | C | D | E | F | G | H | I | J |
|---|---|---|---|---|---|---|---|---|---|---|
| Kakaris | G | G | G | G | — | — | — | — | — | — |
| Christidis | — | — | — | — | G | G | — | — | — | — |
| Constantinou | — | — | — | — | — | — | G | G | G | G |
| Kyrastas | RB | RB | RB | RB | — | RB | RB | RB | — | — |
| Pallas | — | — | — | — | RB[1] | RCB | LB | — | — | — |
| Karavitis | — | — | — | RH[2] | RB[2] | — | — | — | — | — |
| Xantopoulos | — | — | — | — | — | — | — | — | RB | CH[2] |
| Ziakos | — | — | — | — | — | — | CF[2] | — | LH[2] | RB |
| Foiros | RCB | RCB | RCB | RCB | LCB | LCB | RCB | LCB | LCB | LCB |
| Nikolaou | — | — | — | — | RCB | — | — | — | — | — |
| Kapsis | — | — | — | — | — | — | — | — | — | RCB |
| Ravousis | LCB | LCB | LCB | LCB[1] | — | LB | LCB | RCB | RCB | — |
| Pellios | — | — | — | LCB[2] | — | — | — | — | — | — |
| Iosifidis | LB | LB | LB | LB | LB | — | — | LB | LB | LB |
| Anastasiadis | RH[1] | RH | RH | CH | — | — | — | — | — | — |
| Semerzidis | RH[2] | — | LH[2] | — | RF[2] | — | RF[2] | — | — | — |
| Tersanidis | — | — | — | RH[1] | RH | RH | — | — | — | — |
| Damanakis | CH | CH | CH | — | CH | CH | — | CH[2] | RH | — |
| Delikaris | — | — | — | — | — | CF | LH | CH[1] | CF | LH |
| Koudas | — | — | — | — | — | — | — | LH | — | CH[1] |
| Nikoloudis | LH[1] | — | LH[1] | — | — | LH | CH | RH | LH[1] | RH |
| Papaioannou | LH[2] | LH | — | LH | LH | — | — | — | — | — |
| Ardizoglou | RF | — | RF | RF[1] | RF[1] | — | RH | RF[1] | CH | LF |
| Kalakadas | — | RF | — | — | — | — | — | — | — | — |
| Orphanos | — | — | CF[2] | RF[2] | — | — | — | — | — | — |
| Mitropoulos | — | — | — | — | — | RF | RF[1] | RF[2] | — | — |
| Galakous | CF | CF | CF[1] | CF | CF | — | CF[1] | CF | RF | CF |
| Infandidis | — | — | — | — | — | — | — | — | — | RF |
| Mavros | LF | LF | LF | LF | LF | LF | LF | LF | LF | — |

# NORTHERN IRELAND

A 13. 5. 78 Scotland .................... 1 (Johnstone) — Northern Ireland ........... 1 (O'Neill) — Glasgow (BHC)
B 16. 5. 78 England .................... 1 (Neal) — Northern Ireland ........... 0 — Wembley (BHC)
C 19. 5. 78 Wales ...................... 1 (Deacy) — Northern Ireland ........... 0 — Wrexham (BHC)
D 20. 9. 78 Rep. of Ireland ............. 0 — Northern Ireland ........... 0 — Dublin (EFC)
E 25. 10. 78 Northern Ireland ........... 2 (Spence, Anderson) — Denmark .................. 1 (H. Jensen) — Belfast (EFC)
F 29. 11. 78 Bulgaria .................... 0 — Northern Ireland ........... 2 (Armstrong, Caskey) — Sofia (EFC)

| | A | B | C | **D | E | F |
|---|---|---|---|---|---|---|
| Platt | G | G | G | — | — | — |
| Jennings | — | — | — | G | G | G |
| B. Hamilton | RB | RB | RB | RCB[2] | — | RB |
| Rice | — | — | — | RB | RB | — |
| C. Nicholl | RCB | RCB | RCB | LCB | — | LCB |
| J. Nicholl | LCB | LCB | LCB | LCH | RCB | RCB |
| Hunter | — | — | — | RCB[1] | LCB | — |
| Scott | LB | LB | LB[1] | — | — | — |
| Nelson | — | — | LB[2] | LB | LB | LB |
| O' Neill | RH | RH | RH | RH | RH | RH |
| McCreery | CH | CH | CH | RCH | CH | CH |

**4-4-2

| | A | B | C | **D | E | F |
|---|---|---|---|---|---|---|
| McIlroy | LH | LH | LH | LH | LH | LH[1] |
| Moreland | — | — | — | — | — | LH[2] |
| Anderson | RF[1] | RF | RF[1] | — | CF[3] | — |
| W. Hamilton | RF[2] | — | — | — | — | — |
| Armstrong | CF | CF | CF | RF | RF | RF |
| Spence | — | — | — | LF[1] | CF[2] | — |
| Morgan | — | — | — | — | CF[1] | — |
| McGrath | LF[1] | LF[1] | LF | — | — | LF[2] |
| Cochrane | LF[2] | LF[2] | RF[2] | LF[2] | LF | LF[1] |
| Caskey | — | — | — | — | — | CF |

# REPUBLIC OF IRELAND

A 5. 4. 78 Republic of Ireland ......... 4 (Treacy 2, Giles, McGee) — Turkey ..................... 2 (Onder, Cemil) — Dublin
B 12. 4. 78 Poland .................... 3 (Boniek, Deyna, Mazur) — Republic of Ireland ......... 0 — Lodz
C 21. 5. 78 Norway .................... 0 — Republic of Ireland ......... 0 — Oslo
D 24. 5. 78 Denmark ................... 3 (Jensen, Nielsen, Lerby) — Republic of Ireland ......... 3 (Stapleton, Grealish, G. Daly) — Copenhagen (EFC)
E 20. 9. 78 Republic of Ireland ......... 0 — Northern Ireland ........... 0 — Dublin (EFC)
F 25. 10. 78 Republic of Ireland ......... 1 (G. Daly) — England ..................... 1 (Latchford) — Dublin (EFC)

| | A | **B | C | D | E | F |
|---|---|---|---|---|---|---|
| Peyton | G | G | — | — | — | — |
| Kearns | — | — | G | G | G | G |
| Langan | RB | — | RB[1] | — | — | — |
| Gregg | — | RB | — | LB[2] | — | RCB[2] |
| Lawrenson | — | RCB | RB[2] | RCB | LCB | LCB |
| Mulligan | — | — | LCB | RB | RB | RB |
| Synnott | RCB | LCB | — | — | RCB | — |
| O'Leary | — | — | RCB | LCB | — | RCB[1] |
| Holmes | LCB | LB | LB | LB[1] | LB | LB |
| M. Daly | LB | RH | — | — | — | — |
| G. Daly | RH[1] | — | — | LH | LH | RH |
| Braddish | RH[2] | LCH | — | — | — | — |
| Grealish | | — | RH | RH | RB | CH |

**4-4-2

| | A | **B | C | D | E | F |
|---|---|---|---|---|---|---|
| Giles | CH | RCH[1] | CH | CH | CH | — |
| Clarke | — | RCH[2] | — | — | — | — |
| Grimes | LH | LH | LH[2] | — | — | — |
| Brady | — | — | LH[1] | — | LH | LH |
| McGee | RF | — | LF[2] | LF[2] | CF | RF[1] |
| Treacy | CF | RF | — | — | — | — |
| Heighway | — | — | RF | RF | RF[1] | — |
| Givens | — | — | LF[1] | LF[1] | RF[2] | CF |
| Stapleton | — | — | CF | CF | LF[1] | RF[2] |
| Ryan | LF | — | — | — | — | LF |
| Mucklan | — | LF | — | — | — | — |
| Walsh | — | — | — | — | LF[2] | — |

# ITALY

| | Date | Home | | Away | | Venue |
|---|---|---|---|---|---|---|
| A | 25. 1. 78 | Spain (Pirri, Dani) | 2 | Italy (Tardelli) | 1 | Madrid |
| B. | 8. 2. 78 | Italy (Graziani 2) | 2 | France (Bathenay, Platini) | 2 | Naples |
| C | 18. 5. 78 | Italy | 0 | Yugoslavia | 0 | Rome |
| D | 2. 6. 78 | Italy (Rossi, Zaccarelli) | 2 | France (Lacombe) | 1 | Mar del Plata (WC) |
| E | 6. 6. 78 | Italy (Rossi, Bettega, Benetti) | 3 | Hungary (A.Toth) | 1 | Mar del Plata (WC) |
| F | 10. 6. 78 | Argentina | 0 | Italy (Bettega) | 1 | Buenos Aires (WC) |
| G | 14. 6. 78 | Italy | 0 | West Germany | 0 | Buenos Aires (WC) |
| H | 18. 6. 78 | Italy (Rossi) | 1 | Austria | 0 | Buenos Aires (WC) |
| I | 21. 6. 78 | Netherlands (Brandts, Haan) | 2 | Italy (one o.g.) | 1 | Buenos Aires (WC) |
| J | 24. 6. 78 | Brazil (Nelinho, Dirceu) | 2 | Italy (Causio) | 1 | Buenos Aires (WC) |
| K | 20. 9. 78 | Italy (Cabrini) | 1 | Bulgaria | 0 | Turin |
| L | 24. 9. 78 | Italy (Graziani) | 1 | Turkey | 0 | Florence |
| M | 8. 11. 78 | Czechoslovakia (Jarusek, Panenka, Masny) | 3 | Italy | 0 | Bratislava |
| N | 21. 12. 78 | Italy (Rossi) | 1 | Spain | 0 | Rome |

| | A | B | C | D | E | F | G | H | I | J | K | L | M | N |
|---|---|---|---|---|---|---|---|---|---|---|---|---|---|---|
| Conti | G | — | — | — | — | — | — | — | — | — | — | G | — | G[2] |
| Zoff | — | G | G | G | G | G | G | G | G | G | G | — | G | G[1] |
| Gentile | RB | RB | RB | RB | RB | RB | RB | RB | LCB | LCB | RB | LB | RB | RB |
| Scirea | RCB[1] | RCB | RCB | RCB | RCB | RCB | RCB | RCB | RCB | RCB | RCB | LCB[1] | RCB | RCB |
| Bellugi | RCB[2] | LCB | LCB | LCB | LCB | LCB[1] | LCB | LCB[1] | — | — | LCB | LCB[2] | LCB | LCB[1] |
| Cuccureddu | — | — | — | — | LB[2] | LCB[2] | — | LCB[2] | RB | RB | — | RB[1] | — | LCB[2] |
| Maldera | LB | LB | LB | — | — | — | — | — | — | CH | — | — | — | — |
| Cabrini | — | — | — | LB | LB[1] | LB | LB | LB | LB | LB | LB | RB[2] | LB | LB |
| Manfredonia | LCB | — | — | — | — | — | — | — | — | — | — | RCB | — | — |
| P. Sala | RH | LH[2] | — | — | — | — | — | — | — | LH | — | RH[1] | — | — |
| Benetti | — | RH | RH | CH | RH | CH | CH | CH | CH[1] | — | CH | CH[1] | RH | RH |
| Antognoni | LH[1] | LH[1] | — | RH[1] | LH | LH[1] | LH[1] | — | — | RH[1] | RH | LH | LH | — |
| Zaccarelli | LH[2] | — | CF | RH[2] | — | LH[2] | LH[2] | LH | RH | — | — | — | — | — |
| Tardelli | RCH | CH | LH | LH | CH | RH | RH | RH | LH | — | LH | RH[2] | CH[1] | LH |
| Pecci | — | — | — | — | — | — | — | — | — | — | — | CH[2] | — | — |
| C. Sala | LCH | RF | — | — | — | — | — | — | RF[2] | RH[2] | — | — | CH[2] | — |
| Rossi | RF | — | — | CF | CF | CF | CF | CF | CF | CF | — | — | CF | RF |
| Graziani | — | CF | RF | — | LF[2] | — | — | LF[2] | CH[2] | — | CF | GF[1] | LF[2] | LF |
| Causio | — | — | CH | RF | RF | RF | RF | RF | RF[1] | RF | RF | RF[1] | RF | CH |
| Novellino | — | — | — | — | — | — | — | — | — | — | — | RF[2] | — | — |
| Pruzzo | — | — | — | — | — | — | — | — | — | — | — | CF[2] | — | — |
| Bettega | — | LF[1] | LF | LF | LF[1] | LF | LF | LF[1] | LF | LF | LF | — | LF[1] | — |
| Pulici | LF | LF[2] | — | — | — | — | — | — | — | — | — | LF | — | — |
| Giordano | — | — | — | — | — | — | — | — | — | — | — | — | — | CF |

# NETHERLANDS

| | Date | Home | | Away | | Venue |
|---|---|---|---|---|---|---|
| A | 22. 2. 78 | Israel (Peretz) | 1 | Netherlands (Rensenbrink, Tscheu La Ling | 2 | Tel Aviv |
| B | 5. 4. 78 | Tunisia | 0 | Netherlands (Nanninga 2, Leeuwen one o.g.) | 4 | Tunis |
| C | 20. 5. 78 | Austria | 0 | Netherlands (Haan) | 1 | Vienna |
| D | 3. 6. 78 | Netherlands (Rensenbrink 3) | 3 | Iran | 0 | Mendoza (WC) |
| E | 7. 6. 78 | Netherlands | 0 | Peru | 0 | Mendoza (WC) |
| F | 11. 6. 78 | Scotland (Gemmill 2, Dalglish) | 3 | Netherlands (Rensenbrink, Rep) | 2 | Mendoza (WC) |
| G | 14 6. 78 | Netherlands (Brandts, Rensenbrink Rep 2, W. van der Kerkhof) | 5 | Austria (Obermayer) | 1 | Cordoba (WC) |
| H | 18. 6. 78 | Netherlands (Haan, R. van der Kerkhof) | 2 | West Germany (Abramczik, D. Muller) | 2 | Cordoba (WC) |
| I | 21. 6. 78 | Netherlands (Brandts, Haan) | 2 | Italy (one o.g.) | 1 | Buenos Aires (WC) |
| J | 25. 6. 78 | Argentina (Kempes 2, Bertoni) | 3 | Netherlands (Nanninga) | 1 | Buenos Aires (World Cup Final) |
| K | 20. 9. 78 | Netherlands (Krol, Brandts, Rensenbrink) | 3 | Iceland | 0 | Nijmegen (EFC) |
| L | 11. 10. 78 | Switzerland (Tanner) | 1 | Netherlands (Wildschut, Brandts, Geels) | 3 | Berne (EFC) |
| M | 15. 11. 78 | Netherlands (Geels 2, one o.g.) | 3 | East Germany | 0 | Rotterdam (EFC) |
| N | 20 12. 78 | West Germany (Rummenigge, Fischer, Bonhof) | 3 | Netherlands (Tscheu La Ling) | 1 | Dusseldorf |

| | A | B | **C | **D | E | F | G | **H | I | **J | K | L | M | N |
|---|---|---|---|---|---|---|---|---|---|---|---|---|---|---|
| Schrijvers | G | — | — | — | — | — | G | G | G[1] | — | G | G | G | G |
| Jongbloed | — | G | G | G | G | G | — | — | G[2] | G | — | — | — | — |
| Suurbier | RB | RB | RB | RB | RB | RB | — | — | — | RB[2] | — | — | — | — |
| Wildschut | — | LB | — | — | — | LCB[2] | RB | LB[1] | — | — | LCB | LCB | RH | — |
| Poortvliet | — | — | LB | — | LB | LB | LB | RB | RB | LB | RB | RB | — | RB |
| van Kraay | — | RCB | — | — | — | — | LCB[2] | — | RF[2] | — | — | — | RB | — |
| Krol | RCB | LCB | RCB | RCB | LCB | RCB | RCB | LCB | LCB | LCB | RCB | RCB | RCB | RCB[1] |
| Rijsbergen | LCB | — | LCB | LCB | RCB | LCB[1] | — | — | — | — | — | — | — | — |
| Brandts | — | — | — | — | — | — | LCB[1] | RCB | LB | RCB | LB | LB | LCB | LCB |
| Metgod | — | — | — | — | — | — | — | — | — | — | — | — | CH[2] | RCB[2] |
| Hovenkamp | LB | — | — | — | — | — | — | — | — | — | — | LH[1] | LB | LB |
| W. van der Kerkhof | RH | RH[1] | LH[1] | LB | CF | LH | LH | LH | RCB | LCB | LH | RH[1] | — | LH |
| R. van der Kerkhof | LH[2] | RH[2] | RF[2] | LH[1] | RF[1] | RF | CF[1] | RH | CF | LH | — | — | RF[1] | — |
| Neeskens | — | — | RH | RH | RH[1] | RH[1] | — | — | RH | RH | — | — | CH[1] | CH |
| Boskamp | — | — | — | — | — | RH[2] | — | — | — | — | — | — | — | — |
| Jansen | CH[2] | CH | RCH | LCH | CH | CH | RH | LCH | CH | RB[1] | RH | — | — | RH |
| Haan | — | — | LH[2] | RCH | LH | — | CH | RCH | LH | RCH | CH | CH | — | — |
| Peters | CH[1] | — | — | — | — | — | — | — | — | — | — | RH[2] | LH | — |
| van Hanegem | LH[1] | — | LCH | — | — | — | — | — | — | — | — | — | — | — |
| Muehren | — | LH | — | — | — | — | — | — | — | — | — | — | — | — |
| Dusbaba | — | — | — | — | — | — | — | — | — | — | — | LH[2] | — | — |
| Tscheu La Ling | RF | — | — | — | — | — | — | — | — | — | — | — | — | RF |
| van Leeuwen | CF | RF | — | — | — | — | — | — | — | — | — | — | — | — |
| Rep | — | — | RF[1] | RF | RF[2] | CF | RF | RF | RF[1] | RF[1] | — | — | — | CF |
| Nanninga | — | CF | — | LH[2] | RH[2] | — | — | LB[2] | — | RF[2] | CF | CF | — | — |
| Koster | — | — | — | — | — | — | — | — | — | — | RF | — | RF[2] | LF[1] |
| Geels | — | — | — | — | — | — | — | — | — | — | — | RF | CF | — |
| Schoenaker | — | — | — | — | — | — | CF[2] | — | — | — | — | — | — | — |
| Rensenbrink | LF | — | LF | LF | LF | LF | LF | LF | LF | LF | LF | LF | LF | — |
| Vermeulen | — | LF | — | — | — | — | — | — | — | — | — | — | — | LF[2] |

** 4-4-2

# SOVIET UNION

| |  | | | |
|---|---|---|---|---|
| A | 26. 2. 78 | Morocco .......... 2<br>(Scherif, Asila) | Soviet Union .......... 3<br>(Blochin, Konkov, Chesnokov) | — Marrakesh |
| B | 8. 3. 78 | West Germany .......... 1<br>(Russmann) | Soviet Union .......... 0 | — Frankfurt |
| C | 5. 4. 78 | Soviet Union .......... 10<br>(Blochin 4, Konkov, Kolotov 2, Kipiani, Chesnokov, Petrakov) | Finland .......... 2<br>(Heiskanen, Nieminen) | — Erevan |
| D | 14. 5. 78 | Rumania .......... 0 | Soviet Union .......... 1<br>(Blochin) | — Bucharest |
| E | 6. 9. 78 | Iran .......... 0 | Soviet Union .......... 1<br>(Chidijatulin) | — Tehran |
| F | 20. 9. 78 | Soviet Union .......... 2<br>(Chesnokov, Bessonov) | Greece .......... 0 | — Erevan (EFC) |
| G | 4. 10. 78 | Turkey .......... 0 | Soviet Union .......... 2<br>(Gusajev, Blochin) | — Ankara |
| H | 11. 10. 78 | Hungary .......... 2<br>(Varadi, Szokolai) | Soviet Union .......... 0 | — Budapest (EFC) |

| | A | B | ***C | D | E | F | G | H |
|---|---|---|---|---|---|---|---|---|
| Degtjarev | G$^{1}$ | G | G$^{1}$ | G$^{1}$ | G | G | — | G$^{1}$ |
| Novikov | G$^{2}$ | — | G$^{2}$ | — | — | — | — | — |
| Gontar | — | — | — | G$^{2}$ | — | — | G | G$^{2}$ |
| Prigoda | RB | RB | RB | RB | RB | RB | — | — |
| Zupikov | RCB | LCB | CB | RCB | RCB | RCB | RCB | RCB |
| Bubnov | — | RCB | — | LCB | LCB | LCB | LCB | LCB |
| Golubjev | LCB | — | LB | — | — | — | — | — |
| Machovikov | LB | LB | — | LB | LB | — | LB | LB |
| Konkov | — | RH | RH | CH | RH | LB | RB | RB |
| Burjak | RH | LH$^{1}$ | RCF$^{2}$ | — | LH | CH | CH | LH$^{1}$ |
| Bereznoj | — | LH$^{2}$ | — | RH | — | RH | RH | RH |
| Bessonov | CH | — | LCF | CF | CF | CF | LH | CH |
| Veremejev | CF | CH | RCF$^{1}$ | — | — | — | — | — |
| Petrakov | — | — | CH$^{2}$ | LH$^{2}$ | — | — | — | — |
| Chidijatulin | — | — | — | — | CH | LH | CF$^{1}$ | CF |
| Kipiani | LH | — | LH | LH$^{1}$ | — | — | — | — |
| Jarcev | — | — | — | — | RF$^{1}$ | — | CF$^{2}$ | LH$^{2}$ |
| Kolotov | RF$^{1}$ | RF$^{1}$ | OR | RF$^{2}$ | — | — | — | — |
| Chesnokov | RF$^{2}$ | RF$^{2}$ | CH$^{1}$ | — | — | RF | LF$^{2}$ | — |
| Fedotov | — | — | — | RF$^{1}$ | — | — | — | — |
| Gusajev | — | — | — | — | RF$^{2}$ | — | RF | RF |
| Fjodorov | — | CF$^{1}$ | — | — | — | — | — | — |
| Minaev | — | CF$^{2}$ | — | — | — | — | — | — |
| Blochin | LF | LF | OL | LF | LF | LF | LF$^{1}$ | LF |

*** 3-3-4

# PORTUGAL

| |  | | | |
|---|---|---|---|---|
| A | 8. 3. 78 | France .......... 2<br>(Baronchelli, Berdoll) | Portugal .......... 0 | — Paris |
| B | 21. 9. 78 | Portugal .......... 1<br>(Costa) | U.S.A. .......... 0 | — Setubal |
| C | 11 10. 78 | Portugal .......... 1<br>(Gomes) | Belgium .......... 1<br>(Vercautern) | — Lisbon (EFC) |
| D | 15. 11. 78 | Austria .......... 1<br>(Schachner) | Portugal .......... 2<br>(Nene, Alberto) | — Vienna (EFC) |
| E | 29. 11. 78 | Portugal .......... 1<br>(Costa) | Scotland .......... 0 | — Lisbon (EFC) |

| | **A | B | C | **D | E |
|---|---|---|---|---|---|
| Bento | G | G | G | G | G |
| Artur | RB | — | RH[2] | RB | RB |
| Gabriel | — | RB | RB | — | — |
| Cardoso | RCB | — | — | — | — |
| Alhinho | — | RCB[1] | — | RCB | LCB |
| Eurico | — | RCB[2] | RCB | — | LH[2] |
| Humberto | LCB | LCB | LCB | LCB | RCB |
| Laranjeia | LB | — | — | — | — |
| Oliveira | RH | LB | CH | LH | LH[1] |
| Teixeira | — | — | LB | RCH | — |
| Alberto | — | — | — | LB | LB |
| Alves | LH | RH | LH | LCH | CH |

** 4-4-2

| | **A | B | C | **D | E |
|---|---|---|---|---|---|
| Sheu | — | CH | RH[1] | — | RF[2] |
| Pietra | — | LF | — | RH | RH |
| Toni | RCH | — | — | — | — |
| Celso | LCH | — | — | — | — |
| M. Fernandez | LF[1] | LH[1] | CF[1] | — | — |
| Nene | — | LH[2] | CF[2] | CF | LF |
| Costa | RF[1] | CF[1] | RF | RF | RF[1] |
| Oscar | RF[2] | — | — | — | — |
| Gomes | — | RF | LF | — | CF |
| Seninho | LF[2] | — | — | — | — |
| Chalana | — | CF[2] | — | — | — |

# SWITZERLAND

| | Date | Home | | Away | | Venue |
|---|---|---|---|---|---|---|
| A | 8. 3. 78 | East Germany (Hoffmann 2, Riediger) | 3 | Switzerland (Sulser) | 1 | Karl Marx Stadt |
| B | 4. 4. 78 | Switzerland | 0 | Austria (Jara) | 1 | Basle |
| C | 6. 9. 78 | Switzerland (Elsener, Schynder) | 2 | U.S.A. | 0 | Lucerne |
| D | 11. 10. 78 | Switzerland (Tanner) | 1 | Netherlands (Wildschut, Brandts, Geels) | 3 | Berne(EFC) |
| E | 15. 11. 78 | Poland (Boniek, Ogaza) | 2 | Switzerland | 0 | Wroclaw (EFC) |

| | **A | B | **C | D | **E |
|---|---|---|---|---|---|
| Burgener | G | G | G[1] | G | — |
| Engel | — | — | G[2] | — | G |
| Parietti | RB | — | — | — | — |
| Wehrli | LH | RB | RH | CH[2] | — |
| Brechbuhl | — | — | RB | RB | RB |
| Chapuisat | RCB | RCB | RCB | RCB | RCB |
| Stohler | LCB | — | — | — | — |
| Montandon | — | LCB | LCB | LCB | LCB |
| Fischbach | LB | LB | LB[2] | — | — |
| Bizzini | — | — | LB[1] | LB | LB |

**4-4-2

| | **A | B | **C | D | **E |
|---|---|---|---|---|---|
| Botteron | RH | LH | LH[1] | LF | RCH |
| Meyer | — | RH | — | — | LCH |
| Barberis | RCH | CH | — | RH | RH |
| Gross | LCH | — | — | — | — |
| Schynder | — | — | LCH | LH[1] | LH |
| Tanner | — | — | — | CH[1] | — |
| Hermann | — | — | LH[2] | — | — |
| Sulser | RF | RF | RF | RF | RF |
| Ponte | — | CF | RCH | LH[2] | LF[2] |
| Elsener | LF | LF | LF | CF | LF[1] |

# SCOTLAND

| | Date | Home | | Away | | Venue |
|---|---|---|---|---|---|---|
| A | 22. 2. 78 | Scotland (Gemmill, Wallace) | 2 | Bulgaria (Mladenov) | 1 | — Glasgow |
| B | 13. 5. 78 | Scotland (Johnstone) | 1 | Northern Ireland (O' Neill) | 1 | — Glasgow (BHC) |
| C | 17. 5. 78 | Scotland (Johnstone) | 1 | Wales (Donachie o.g.) | 1 | — Glasgow (BHC) |
| D | 20. 5. 78 | Scotland | 0 | England (Coppell) | 1 | — Glasgow (BHC) |
| E | 3. 6. 78 | Peru (Cueto, Cubillas 2) | 3 | Scotland (Jordan) | 1 | — Cordoba (WC) |
| F | 7. 6. 78 | Scotland (Eskandarian o.g.) | 1 | Iran (Danaifar) | 1 | — Cordoba (WC) |
| G | 11. 6. 78 | Scotland (Dalglish, Gemmill 2) | 3 | Netherlands (Rensenbrink, Rep) | 2 | — Mendoza (WC) |
| H | 20. 9. 78 | Austria (Pezzey, Schachner, Kreuz) | 3 | Scotland (McQueen, A. Gray) | 2 | — Vienna (EFC) |
| I | 25. 10.78 | Scotland (Dalglish 2, Gemmill) | 3 | Norway (E. Aas, Okland) | 2 | — Glasgow (EFC) |
| J | 29. 11. 78 | Portugal (Costa) | 1 | Scotland | 0 | — Lisbon (EFC) |

| | **A | B | C | D | E | F | **G | H | I | J |
|---|---|---|---|---|---|---|---|---|---|---|
| Blyth | G | — | G | — | — | — | — | — | — | — |
| Rough | — | G | — | G | G | G | G | G | — | G |
| J. Stewart | — | — | — | — | — | — | — | — | G | — |
| Kennedy | RB | — | RB | RB | RB | — | RB | RB | — | RB |
| Jardine | — | RB | — | — | — | RB | — | — | — | — |
| McQueen | RCB | LCB | RCB$^{1}$ | — | — | — | — | RCB | RCB | RCB |
| Forsyth | — | RCB | RCB$^{2}$ | LCB | RCB | LCB$^{2}$ | RCB | — | — | — |
| Burns | — | LB$^{2}$ | LCB | RCB | LCB | RCB | — | — | — | — |
| Miller | LCB | — | — | — | — | — | — | — | — | — |
| Buchan | — | LB$^{1}$ | — | — | LB | LCB$^{1}$ | LCB | LCB | LCB | LCB |
| Donachie | LB | — | LB | LB | — | LB | LB | LB | RB | LB$^{2}$ |
| F. Gray | — | — | — | — | — | — | — | — | LB | LB$^{1}$ |
| Souness | RH | — | RH | CH$^{2}$ | — | — | LH | CH | CH | — |
| Rioch | — | RH | — | RH$^{1}$ | RH$^{1}$ | — | RH | — | — | — |
| Macari | RCH | — | — | — | RH$^{2}$ | CH | — | — | — | — |
| Gemmill | LCH | LH | CH | RH$^{2}$ | LH$^{2}$ | RH | RCH | RH | RH | RH |
| Masson | — | CH | — | CH$^{1}$ | LH$^{1}$ | — | — | — | — | — |
| Hartford | LH | — | LH | LH | CH | LH | LCH | LH | LH | LH |
| Narey | — | — | — | — | — | — | — | — | — | CH |
| Jordan | RF$^{1}$ | RF$^{1}$ | — | CF | CF | CF | LF | LF$^{1}$ | — | CF$^{1}$ |
| D. Johnstone | RF$^{2}$ | CF | RF | — | — | — | — | — | — | — |
| Dalglish | LF$^{1}$ | RF$^{2}$ | CF | RF | RF | RF$^{1}$ | RF | RF | RF | RF |
| Wallace | LF$^{2}$ | — | — | — | — | — | — | — | — | CF$^{2}$ |
| Robertson | — | LF | LF$^{2}$ | — | — | LF | — | — | — | LF |
| Johnston | — | — | LF$^{1}$ | LF | LF | — | — | — | — | — |
| A. Gray | — | — | — | — | — | — | — | CF | CF | — |
| Harper | — | — | — | — | — | RF$^{2}$ | — | — | — | — |
| Graham | — | — | — | — | — | — | — | LF$^{2}$ | LF | — |

** 4-4-2